EXPLORING
CAREERS

Careers in Sports and Fitness

Debra Schmidt

ReferencePoint
Press®

About the Author

Debra Schmidt is the author of English language learner
curriculum for *Disney English* and science curriculum for Scott
Foresman, UC Irvine's California Science Implementation
Network, Wildlife Education, and Scantron. She lives in San
Diego with her family.

For more information, contact:
ReferencePoint Press, Inc.
PO Box 27779
San Diego, CA 92198
www.ReferencePointPress.com

Picture Credits:
 6: Maury Aaseng
11: Jakkrit Orrasri/Shutterstock.com
18: Michael Jung/Thinkstock Images
27: Highwaystarz Photography/Thinkstock Images
60: Marcio Jose Bastos Silva/Shutterstock.com

LIBRARY OF CONGRESS CATALOGING-IN-PUBLICATION DATA

Names: Schmidt, Debra.
Title: Careers in sports and fitness / by Debra Schmidt.
Description: San Diego, CA : ReferencePoint Press, Inc., 2016. | Series: Exploring careers | Includes
    bibliographical references and index.
Identifiers: LCCN 2015030317| ISBN 9781601528148 (hardback) | ISBN 1601528140 (hardback)
Subjects: LCSH: Sports--Vocational guidance--United States--Juvenile literature. | Physical
    fitness--Vocational guidance--United States--Juvenile literature.
Classification: LCC GV734.3 .S36 2016 | DDC 796.023--dc23 LC record available at
    http://lccn.loc.gov/2015030317

Contents

Satisfying and Fast-Growing Careers

The most prominent people working in sports and fitness are professional athletes, but they represent a small fraction of those employed in this field. According to the CareerBuilder website, as of 2014 the total number of professional athletes employed in all sports was just 9,775. In contrast, the same site reports, the top sports and fitness career fields (which include sports teams and clubs, sports promoters, racetracks, other spectator sports, and agents and managers) accounted for about 350,000 jobs. Within these industries 147,921 people worked in auxiliary sports-related careers. These include event planners, audio and video equipment technicians, market research analysts and marketing specialists, laborers, freight and stock movers, radio and television announcers, ushers, ticket takers, security guards, coaches, and scouts.

Careers in sports and fitness are among the fastest-growing occupations in the United States. The demand for sports-related careers has increased due to a booming sports and fitness industry, high rates of child and adult obesity, an aging population, increased interest in leisure sports, innovative sports technologies, and mounting evidence on the benefits of exercise. According to the Plunkett Research website, the total US sports and fitness market generates $485 billion per year, which fuels hundreds of different sports and fitness jobs. In the CareerBuilder article "22 of the Fastest Growing Sports Jobs," journalist Debra Auerbach writes that sports-related industries grew by 12.6 percent between 2010 and 2014, but the total national job market increased by only 5.5 percent.

From Passion to Profession

Many people choose a career in sports or fitness to channel their passion for recreational activities, healthy habits, and exercise into a rewarding profession. Opportunities for making a difference in people's lives abound. According to the American Heart Association, about 31 percent (23.9 million) of American children and 35 percent (78 million) of adults are overweight or obese. Recreation workers, PE teachers, sports dietitians, personal trainers, fitness instructors, and others in this field are well positioned to help people from all walks of life develop positive exercise and eating habits. According to Manuel Gonzalez, a San Diego Park and Recreation Department district manager, "Recreation workers are positioned to be a key part of the obesity epidemic solution by integrating healthy habits, exercise, nutrition, and sports into recreation centers, especially to youth in low income and disadvantaged areas."

Diverse Career Options

Sports and fitness careers are diverse, with a job for every interest. Those interested in working directly with athletes can become athletic trainers, coaches, umpires, sports psychologists, or agents. Those wanting to work for a team might choose work in publicity, sports event planning, or media relations; likewise, they can find office jobs such as accountants, secretaries, and bookkeepers. There are also numerous service-sector jobs, including ticket sales, concessions, and merchandise sales. Those interested in research, design, science, or engineering can find rewarding career choices in the sports and fitness field. Sports foods, drinks, and supplements are big businesses in America. Scientists, sales personnel, and sports dietitians are well-paying careers in the field of nutrition research. Each year amateur and professional athletes purchase the newest sports equipment and apparel. People with a flair for design can channel their creative talents into designing sports clothing and shoes. Sports engineers are needed to design and test equipment for every sport. There are many sports and fitness career paths for those interested in science, such as

Careers in Sports and Fitness

Occupational Title	Employment, 2012	Projected Employment, 2022	Percent Increase
Athletes and Sports Competitors	14,900	15,900	7 percent
Athletic Trainers	22,900	27,800	21 percent
Coaches and Scouts	243,900	280,100	15 percent
Dieticians and Nutritionists	67,400	81,600	21 percent
Exercise Physiologists	6,000	6,500	9 percent
Fitness Trainers and Instructors	267,000	300,500	13 percent
Massage Therapists	132,800	162,800	23 percent
Physical Therapist Aides	50,000	70,100	40 percent
Physical Therapist Assistants	71,400	100,700	41 percent
Physical Therapists	204,200	277,700	36 percent
Recreation Workers	345,400	394,400	14 percent
Recreational Therapists	19,800	22,500	13 percent
Umpires, Referees, and Other Sports Officials	17,500	18,800	8 percent

Source: Bureau of Labor Statistics, *Occupational Outlook Handbook*, 2015. www.bls.gov.

being a sports medicine doctor, exercise physiologist, athletic trainer, kinesiotherapist, recreational therapist, and physical therapy assistant. There is a rewarding sports or fitness career to suit every interest and talent.

Satisfying Careers

The highest-paid sports and fitness jobs are generally found in professional sports. A select number of pro athletes earn millions of dollars annually in salaries and lucrative sponsorship deals. American boxer Floyd Mayweather, for instance, is the highest-paid athlete in the world, earning $300 million in 2015. The average pro athlete earns a lot less. The Bureau of Labor Statistics (BLS) reports that professional athletes earn an average salary of $40,060 a year. There are a few other highly paid careers in sports and fitness industries. Those with advanced degrees and extensive training, such as sports medicine physicians, coaches in professional sports, sports administrators, and successful sports entrepreneurs and business owners, can earn salaries in the six figures or higher. For example, Nick Woodman, the creator of the GoPro portable sports camera, is one of the highest-paid executives in America, earning $284.5 million in 2014. According to Ricker, from 2010 through 2014 the majority of sports and fitness employees earned an average of $78,455, which was higher than the national average of $57,947. In an e-mail to the author, Linda Kennedy, a certified personal trainer, supports the idea that people considering a sports and fitness career have realistic ideas about future salaries: "If you think you'll get rich being a trainer, choose a different career. For me, this is a labor of love and my passion—that's what makes me rich!"

Like Kennedy, many people who do these varied jobs describe getting great satisfaction out of their careers. The biggest reward is helping others lead healthier, happier lives. When an athlete or team wins, the fitness professional shares the accomplishment. Whether helping a top-performing athlete win an event or helping a disabled athlete make it to the finish line, these careers offer many personally rewarding experiences. In a phone interview with the author, Barbara Lewin, a certified sports dietitian, commented, "It's not about the money, or having a client that wins the tournament. What I find most rewarding is when a client calls me to say they made a personal best in their sport."

Athletic Trainer

What Does an Athletic Trainer Do?

A high school freshman basketball player was injured during a game and complained of back pain. Doctors cleared him to play, but John Doherty, a certified athletic trainer and now director of the Concussion Clinic in Munster, Illinois, suspected a stress fracture. He referred the student to an orthopedic surgeon who confirmed Doherty's diagnosis. Doherty oversaw the athlete's rehabilitation and full recovery. Athletic trainers like Doherty are health care professionals who work with physicians to prevent, diagnose, manage, and rehabilitate injuries or illnesses in amateur and professional athletes.

Athletic trainers work with people of all ages and abilities. They work with amateur, high school, college, Olympic, and professional athletes. They also work with astronauts, ballerinas, and race car drivers. From treating a skier on the snowy slopes to assisting a surgeon in the operating room to preventing workplace injuries, athletic trainers work in many different settings.

Injury prevention is the key responsibility of athletic trainers. They screen athletes to identify underlying illnesses or injuries. They educate athletes and

At a Glance:
Athletic Trainer

Minimum Educational Requirements

Bachelor's degree

Personal Qualities

Calm in emergencies; strong interpersonal skills

Certification and Licensing

Licensing required in 49 states

Working Conditions

Indoors and outdoors

Salary Range

About $27,610 to $67,070

Number of Jobs

As of 2014, about 22,400

Future Job Outlook

Better than average

coaches about equipment safety. Athletic trainers keep players and staff informed on hydration, nutrition, and wellness issues. They create and implement conditioning programs to reduce injuries and illnesses. Prior to a game, they tape athletes' ankles and wrists to prevent sprains.

An athletic trainer is often the first medical provider to recognize, evaluate, and assess sports injuries. In an article on the Athletic Business website, Jon Almquist, the athletic training administrator for Fairfax County Public Schools in Virginia, says, "We support the concept of the athletic trainer being a healthcare provider who is able to independently deal with 90 percent of the situations that come through the door." Athletic trainers use technology to evaluate injuries. They electronically access the athlete's health record, evaluate data from force sensors in helmets to determine if the athlete has a concussion, and use portable ultrasound devices to look for soft tissue damage. Early diagnosis of concussions and other injuries helps athletes get quick medical treatment.

At sporting events, athletic trainers provide immediate medical care for minor cuts, scrapes, and sprains as well as emergency care for open and closed wounds, head trauma, acute asthma attacks, and other conditions. If they diagnose a serious injury, they follow safety protocol procedures and notify either a doctor or an emergency medical technician.

Most of an athletic trainer's day is spent treating, rehabilitating, and reconditioning athletes. They identify treatment goals and create a treatment plan using hot or cold packs, electrical stimulation, therapeutic ultrasound or laser, mechanical agents like traction, and biofeedback. They use stationary bikes, exercise balls, resistance bands, and other equipment to increase strength, endurance, power, and range of motion. They apply splints, braces, and other assistive devices to speed recovery. Trainers constantly evaluate an athlete's progress, adjusting the treatment plan as needed.

Athletic trainers often work in hospitals and clinics as well as in orthopedic, family practice, pediatric, and sports medicine offices as physician extenders or assistants. In this capacity they take patient histories, evaluate injuries, and report the results to the physician. They also perform routine procedures like removing casts, preparing injections, and fitting patients for crutches or braces.

How Do You Become an Athletic Trainer?

Education

Students who have an interest in becoming a certified athletic trainer should take classes in biology, anatomy, physiology, physics, sports medicine, and physical education. Participation in one or more sports also prepares students for working in the sports and fitness field. Traditionally, those who sought athletic trainer certifications were required to obtain a bachelor's degree from an accredited program. In the future, however, such certification will require a master's degree.

Athletic training programs can be very competitive. This is the case in the athletic training program at the College of Health Sciences at Eastern Kentucky University. Dr. Eric J. Fuchs is the program's director. In an e-mail to the author, Fuchs states, "We have had an average of about 80 to 90 students who are interested in taking prerequisite classes per year but by application time, we usually have about 30 to 34 students apply to the program for 24 slots."

Typical courses include injury prevention, acute care of injury and illness, exercise physiology, and other health-related subjects. As part of college-level coursework, students obtain real-world experiences by completing clinical rotations. These rotations offer supervision and allow students to work directly with patients in health care clinics, hospitals, emergency rooms, or physician's offices. Hands-on learning reinforces the athletic trainer's academic learning and prepares students to diagnose and treat a variety of sports-related injuries and illnesses.

According to the National Athletic Trainers' Association (NATA), "Nearly 70 percent of . . . [certified athletic trainer] credential holders have a master's degree or higher advanced degree." The most popular master's degree programs focus on athletic administration, athletic training, and exercise science; each requires an additional one to three years of study. Athletic training students then can earn a doctorate degree in athletic training, applied physiology and kinesiology, exercise science/biomechanics, and sports medicine by completing an additional one or two years of coursework.

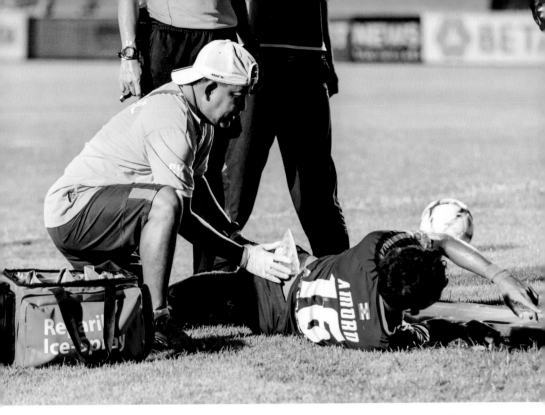

An athletic trainer assists an injured player. Injury prevention is the key responsibility of athletic trainers, but they are often the first to respond to injuries that occur on the field during games and tournaments.

Certification and Licensing

The NATA reports that forty-nine states and the District of Columbia required athletic trainers to be licensed in 2015. (Efforts were under way to require state licensing for athletic trainers in California, the only state that previously has not required licensing for athletic trainers.) The licensing requirements vary by state, so aspiring athletic trainers should consult the state guidelines.

After earning a bachelor's or master's degree from an accredited athletic training program, students must pass the comprehensive Board of Certification exam or a separate state exam. Once they have a job, they must continue their education to maintain their certification.

Volunteer Work and Internships

The best way for students to gain experience in this field is to volunteer with the athletic trainer at their local high school, hospital, college, or university. Due to patient privacy rules, high school students might not be able to work directly with athletes or patients, but they can gain valuable behind-the-scenes insight into many tasks performed in this field. Students may also be able to earn school credit by working as a teacher's assistant to their high school's athletic trainer.

High school students who are interested in athletic training or sports medicine can apply for the Cramer Athletic Training Workshops hosted by the Division of Sports Medicine at the College of William & Mary in Williamsburg, Virginia. Certified athletic trainers from an assortment of work settings conduct lectures and laboratories on emergency first aid; taping and wrapping skills; and the prevention, care, and rehabilitation of athletic injuries.

A variety of organizations—including the Professional Football Athletic Trainers Society, the Mayo School of Health Science, and the sports medicine department at Nationwide Children's Hospital—offer athletic trainer internships to students enrolled in a college-level athletic trainer education program. These internships are competitive because interns work directly with patients and professional athletes.

Skills and Personality

Because athletic trainers are often the first medical providers on the scene of a sports injury, they must have excellent decision-making skills. They use their education and training to diagnose the injury and decide if the athlete is able to return to play, requires basic first aid, or needs immediate care. Because these decisions are often made during a game, trainers need to be professional and calm.

Athletic trainers must have exceptional communication skills. They communicate with athletes, patients, doctors, coaches, and parents. They must be able to explain the diagnosis in terms the patient and/or parent can understand so that the patient will follow through with the treatment plan. They might have to explain complicated medical conditions to coaches and athletes or decide whether to pull an athlete from a game. Listening to the athlete or patient is a key part of an athletic trainer's assessment process.

Compassion is another critical quality. Athletic trainers work closely with patients who are in pain, so they should be patient and gentle. They also work with patients facing serious medical conditions such as diabetes or suffering from life-changing injuries, so they should show empathy and understanding.

On the Job

Employers

High schools, colleges, and universities are the biggest employers of athletic trainers. According to the NATA, about two-thirds of US secondary schools with an athletic program employ athletic trainers either full or part time. Professional sports teams employ at least one—and sometimes several—athletic trainers. Likewise, hospitals, health clinics, and other medical facilities hire athletic trainers. Athletic trainers also work in the arts and entertainment: ballet companies, the Walt Disney Company, and World Wrestling Entertainment all employ athletic trainers to keep their dancers and performers in top condition, prevent injuries, and provide rehabilitative care. Exciting avenues of employment for athletic trainers include working for NASA, the military, and the professional auto racing industry.

Working Conditions

Working conditions for athletic trainers vary. Most athletic trainers work full time, but they may split their work between working with a sports team and working at a physician's office, clinic, or hospital. Athletic trainers working in medical and business settings often work indoors, but they may travel from site to site. Those who work at sporting events or team practices are usually on the sidelines, not far from the action. During training and game season, athletic trainers often work evenings and weekends and must travel to games and events. In an e-mail to the author, Gary Vitti, an athletic trainer for the Los Angeles Lakers with thirty-five years of experience, explained his grueling schedule: "We work 7 days a week most weeks, and about 320 days a year."

Working conditions for athletic trainers can be physically and emotionally challenging. They stand for long periods of time and run, kneel, or crawl while attending to an injured athlete on the field. They may work in inclement weather conditions, including snow, rain, and mud. Athletic trainers employed in urgent care situations may experience the stress that accompanies traumatic injuries. In an article on the website of the Greater Good Science Center at the University of California, Berkeley, athletic trainer Robert McClure writes,

> Constant exposure to pain and suffering is an occupational risk intrinsic to health care. A case may be made that working in high-risk health care settings is similar in some ways to battlefield combat: prolonged stress, risk and complexity that degrades working memory, emotional regulation, and can result in secondary trauma or PTSD [post-traumatic stress disorder].

Earnings

According to the Bureau of Labor Statistics (BLS), as of 2014 the average salary for athletic trainers was $43,370. Athletic trainer salaries are influenced by type of employer, education level, amount of experience, and job location. The highest annual wages for this profession are found in New Jersey, $63,850; the District of Columbia, $63,730; Texas, $54,010; Massachusetts, $51,530; and California, $50,170. Athletic trainer salaries also vary by the type of employer. The BLS reports the annual salary for athletic trainers working in the following industries are elementary and secondary schools, $53,860; spectator sports, $47,070; colleges, universities, and professional schools, $46,860; general medical and surgical hospitals, $45,730; amusement and recreation industries, $43,590; and offices of other health practitioners, $42,630.

Opportunities for Advancement

Assistant athletic trainers who gain work experience and education may advance to management positions as head athletic trainers, athletic directors, or administrators. Trainers may also advance their careers by moving from high school to college and then to professional sports teams. Some athletic trainers capitalize on their expertise by moving into sales and marketing jobs for companies that sell medical and athletic equipment. Athletic trainers who work for colleges and universities usually pursue an advanced degree if they wish to further their careers.

What Is the Future Outlook for Athletic Trainers?

The BLS predicts that employment for athletic trainers will grow 21 percent through 2022, faster than the average for all occupations. The NATA predicts the greatest growth will be in health care settings, such as physician offices and ambulatory or outpatient services. It also anticipates that technological advances and an increased awareness of the benefits of preventive care will expand employment opportunities in elementary and secondary schools. Because turnover is low in this profession, most new jobs will be from job growth rather than from workers retiring.

Find Out More

Board of Certification (BOC)
1415 Harney St., Suite 200
Omaha, NE 68102
phone: (877) 262-3926
website: www.bocatc.org

The BOC provides the only accredited certification program for entry-level athletic trainers. Its website contains information for athletic trainer candidates, including a handbook, news and publications, a blog, and a link to contact information for each state's regulatory agency.

Commission on Accreditation of Athletic Training Education (CAATE)
6850 Austin Center Blvd., Suite 100
Austin, TX 78731-3184
phone: (844) 462-2283
website: http://caate.net

The CAATE is a nonprofit organization dedicated to defining, measuring, and improving athletic training education. The website features informative links for prospective athletic trainers, including how to become an athletic trainer and an educational program search engine.

National Athletic Trainers' Association (NATA)
1620 Valwood Pkwy., Suite 115
Carrollton, TX 75006
phone: (214) 637-6282
website: www.nata.org

The NATA is a worldwide professional association for certified athletic trainers. While much of its website focuses on certified athletic trainers, it has a link for high school and college students with information on financial aid, education, job responsibilities, certification, and employment.

Professional Baseball Athletic Trainers Society (PBATS)
400 Colony Sq., Suite 1750
1201 Peachtree St.
Atlanta, GA 30361
phone: (214) 637-6282
website: www.pbats.com

The PBATS is an educational resource for Major League and Minor League Baseball athletic trainers. The society provides continued education for athletic trainers to improve understanding of sports medicine and to promote the health of professional baseball players. The website has links to jobs, news, a blog, internships, and educational articles on athletic training.

Professional Football Athletic Trainers Society (PFATS)
website: www.pfats.com

The PFATS represents National Football League (NFL) athletic trainers. Its website's member directory provides contact information for athletic trainers employed by each NFL team, links to articles, blogs, scholarships, internships, information about the NFL workplace, and how to become an athletic trainer. It also features articles written by NFL athletic training interns.

Personal Trainer/ Fitness Instructor

What Does a Personal Trainer/ Fitness Instructor Do?

Steve S. (not his real name) took a two-year break from running because of two herniated discs in his back. After he recovered, he set a personal goal to run a marathon but knew he needed help from a personal trainer to reach his goal without reinjuring himself. Linda Kennedy, a certified personal trainer, helped him train for the marathon through stretching, strength and core training, and proper body alignment. Kennedy used her knowledge of body mechanics to monitor Steve during his workouts to ensure he kept his spine properly aligned to prevent injury. With Kennedy's help, Steve finished his first marathon faster than he thought he would, but more importantly he did it injury free.

When people need help achieving personal fitness milestones or with losing weight, staying physically fit, or achieving optimal athletic performance, they often turn to personal trainers

At a Glance:

Personal Trainer/ Fitness Instructor

Minimum Educational Requirements
High school diploma

Personal Qualities
Motivating; physically fit

Certification and Licensing
Personal training or group fitness instructor certification

Working Conditions
Indoors and outdoors

Salary Range
About $18,110 to $67,560

Number of Jobs
As of 2014, about 241,000

Future Job Outlook
Average

A personal trainer urges his client on during a gym workout. Personal trainers, many of whom also work as fitness instructors, help people achieve their individual fitness goals.

and fitness instructors. Many personal trainers also work as fitness instructors and vice versa. These fitness professionals work with clients one-on-one, in small groups, or in scheduled classes to help them achieve their personal fitness goals. They work with clients of all ages and skill levels. They use equipment such as free weights, weight training machines, stability balls, and resistance bands to help clients achieve their fitness goals. They must stay on top of changing ideas about exercise and be aware of developments in fitness equipment.

Personal trainers usually work one-on-one with clients to design a custom workout plan. In the first session or consultation, trainers typically ask questions about the client's health history, current fitness level, and fitness goals. Typical goals include losing weight and increasing strength, flexibility, muscle mass, and endurance. Trainers determine the client's fitness level by taking measurements and having the client perform various exercises. The trainer uses the information gathered at the consultation to create fitness goals and design an exercise plan tailored to the client's desires and fitness level. This custom plan often includes diet recommendations.

Fitness instructors teach structured group exercise classes. These include aerobics, water aerobics, dance, Pilates, yoga, indoor cycling, kickboxing, and weight training. Classes typically include a warm-up, a cooldown, and stretching in addition to the workout. Because fitness instructors do not know the medical histories or fitness levels of participants, they must design classes to meet the group's diverse needs. Teaching group fitness classes is physically challenging, so most instructors work part time, teaching one to ten classes a week. In order to earn a full salary, they often also work as personal trainers or assume administrative positions such as group fitness directors.

An important role of personal trainers and fitness instructors is to teach and monitor clients during workouts. Trainers and instructors demonstrate how to perform exercises and then watch and assist as clients perform the exercise. This might include supervising the use of cardiovascular equipment or spotting clients during weight lifting. Personal trainers also observe and record a client's progress by measuring heart rate, body fat, and number of repetitions. In a group setting, fitness instructors explain and demonstrate modifications for different skill levels. In a yoga class, for example, the instructor will demonstrate a pose for beginning, intermediate, and advanced students, then give feedback to students to help them master the pose. As the client or class progresses over time, the personal trainer or fitness instructor increases the intensity of the workouts so that clients are continually challenged and begin to achieve their goals. This may include increasing weights, repetitions, and exercise time or tackling advanced exercises.

How Do You Become a Personal Trainer/Fitness Instructor?

Education

Students who have an interest in becoming a fitness instructor or personal trainer (or both) should be actively involved in a variety of physical fitness activities. This may include participation in high school or club sports or training in gyms and fitness centers. Taking biology, health science, and psychology is also advised. Some high schools offer vocational training programs, enabling students to complete the classes needed to earn a personal training certificate upon graduation.

There are two educational paths to becoming a personal trainer or group fitness instructor: a traditional two-to-four-year college educational program or a certification program offered by a variety of organizations. According to the Bureau of Labor Statistics (BLS), employers prefer hiring applicants who have earned an associate or bachelor's degree in exercise science, kinesiology, sports medicine, physical education, nutrition, or fitness specialist. An associate degree usually takes two years, and a bachelor's degree requires four years to complete. These programs include health and exercise science, fitness training techniques, business administration, teaching strategies, and nutrition. They may include online lessons, on-campus instruction, and a hands-on internship.

Additional education is required for fitness instructors who teach specialized classes. For example, becoming a yoga teacher requires a two-year program and a minimum of two hundred hours of instruction in anatomy, philosophy, and teaching techniques.

Certification

Most employers require group fitness instructors and personal trainers to be certified, and each has its own certificate. To become certified, applicants must be at least eighteen years old, have a high school diploma or equivalent, and earn both CPR and AED (automated external defibrillator) certifications. They must also pass one or both certification exams depending on whether they plan to work as a fitness instructor, personal trainer, or both.

Certification exams are given by a variety of organizations, including the American Council on Exercise, the National Academy of Sports Medicine, the American College of Sports Medicine, and the National Strength and Conditioning Association. These organizations offer online and home-study certification programs to help applicants prepare for the exam. These study programs are self-paced and students have up to six months to complete the program before the exam. Before enrolling, students should make sure the program is accredited by the National Commission for Certifying Agencies. Each certificate must be renewed every two years. Recertification requirements include keeping CPR and AED certification up to date and completing continuing-education credits.

Volunteer Work and Internships

Students can learn valuable skills by working as a physical education teacher's assistant in their high school weight room, dance program, and track-and-field program. Volunteering at a senior center, youth center, or gym is an excellent way to learn about these careers and gain experience.

Many gyms offer personal training or fitness instructor internships, where interns shadow a professional to get a behind-the-scenes look at daily duties. Internships can be paid or unpaid and also vary in duration. Unpaid internships are usually for current personal training or group fitness instructor students who work under the supervision of a certified professional. The intern observes the mentor in real-life situations to gain practical experience. Paid internships are available to those who are in their final college semesters or recent college graduates. These internships place more responsibility on both the intern and the supervisor. Paid interns receive on-the-job training and perform a variety of jobs under supervision. As the intern gains experience, the tasks become more complicated. 24 Hour Fitness, a nationwide chain of fitness centers, offers internship programs for people interested in becoming a personal trainer or group fitness instructor. According to the 24 Hour Fitness website, mentoring is a key focus of the program:

> You will be mentored by our Fitness Managers, Department Managers and Club Managers, interact and communicate your passion for fitness with our club members and participate in a comprehensive, experiential internship program designed to give you training and a view into what it takes to change people's lives through fitness.

Skills and Personality

The ability to motivate others, a positive attitude, and enthusiasm for helping people achieve their goals are all essential characteristics for anyone who is contemplating work as a personal trainer or fitness instructor. These fitness professionals encourage clients to regularly attend workout sessions or group classes. During workouts they urge clients to push through difficult exercises. On his Tribe Fitness website, Clint Walker, a certified personal trainer, explains the importance of the personal trainer's attitude: "Energy and optimism from your trainer is ESSENTIAL! I like to describe the trainer/client relationship as a mirror. If the trainer is optimistic and energetic, their energy will reflect onto their client."

These professionals are constantly directing individuals and groups, requiring strong communication skills. To be heard across a large room or in a noisy gym, they need to speak slowly, clearly, and with carefully chosen words. Part of being an effective communicator in this field involves constantly assessing clients' comprehension by observing body language and performance. These experts fine-tune the client's technique by giving constructive feedback until the client is able to master the skill.

On the Job

Employers

Personal trainers and fitness instructors are employed by health clubs, yoga and Pilates studios, universities, resorts, country clubs, recreation centers, private businesses, and sometimes by individuals. According to the IBISWorld website, most gyms or fitness centers employ between four and six personal trainers, and large fitness chains like 24 Hour Fitness employ larger numbers of personal trainers and fitness instructors. As the population ages, more retirement homes, senior centers, and organizations are hiring personal trainers and group exercise instructors. For example, San Diego OASIS, a nonprofit organization promoting healthy aging, hired eighty-one-year-old Elinor Smith as a group fitness instructor to teach senior exercise classes. Others are self-employed, operating their own gym or fitness studio.

Working Conditions

Most personal trainers and fitness instructors work indoors at a fitness club or home setting. Increasingly, these fitness professionals are offering individualized and group exercise classes outdoors. Backyard boot camp, beach yoga, stroller-walking classes, and conditioning hikes are popular outdoor classes.

Workload and hours vary. Some personal trainers and group instructors are employed full time and earn a regular salary in commercial, nonprofit, and medical settings. Others are independent contractors working for one or more facilities and are paid per client or per class. Linda Kennedy, a certified personal trainer in San Diego, explains in an e-mail how she handles the fluctuating income when clients cancel appointments: "You need to have a firm financial plan, book about five more appointments than you can perform per week, and you'll hit your goal." Many work weekends, evenings, and split shifts to offer classes during peak times like before and after the standard workday. Many travel to different work settings to accumulate forty hours of work per week.

These professionals are physically active most of their day. They are on their feet or exercising for hours a day, which leads to work-related injuries. Common injuries include repetitive stress or overuse injuries, vocal cord strain, hearing loss, and a variety of foot and knee injuries. This demanding career also contributes to eating disorders and job burnout as individuals face pressure to always look good to impress clients.

Earnings

According to the BLS, personal trainers and fitness instructors earned a median salary of $39,410 in 2014. Personal trainers and fitness instructors who earn a science-related degree earn up to 15 percent more than those without a degree. The BLS reports that the top annual salaries by state for this occupation are New York, $54,050; California, $49,280; New Jersey, $49,030; Connecticut, $48,200; and Massachusetts, $47,260.

Opportunities for Advancement

With experience and additional certifications or a two- to four-year degree, fitness instructors and personal trainers are more likely to be promoted to head trainer, gym manager, or fitness director positions. Many use their education and years of experience to pursue opportunities in sales for nutrition supplements, sports equipment, or apparel companies.

What Is the Future Outlook for Personal Trainers/Fitness Instructors?

The BLS predicts that employment for personal trainers and fitness instructors will increase by about 13 percent through 2022. Those with college degrees are expected to have the best job outlook. Employment growth is attributed to increased public awareness of the benefits of exercise as well as to businesses, government, and insurance organizations offering incentives to employees for joining gyms or taking exercise classes.

Find Out More

American Council on Exercise (ACE)
4851 Paramount Dr.
San Diego, CA 92129
phone: (888) 825-3636
e-mail: support@acefitness.org
website: www.acefitness.org

ACE is committed to America's health and well-being, providing scientific research impacting the fitness industry for fitness professionals and consumers. ACE is the largest nonprofit fitness certification, education, and training organization in the world. Its website contains interviews, articles, public service campaigns, information on the latest research, and consumer health tips.

International Sports Sciences Association (ISSA)
1015 Mark Ave.
Carpinteria, CA 93013
phone: (800) 892-4772
website: www.issaonline.edu

The ISSA provides home study–based and online personal training certification programs as well as continuing-education credits in ninety-one countries. Certifications are recognized worldwide. Its website includes multiple certification programs, a blog, frequently asked questions, a trainer evaluation quiz, health and wellness links, exercise videos, and an income calculator.

National Academy of Sports Medicine (NASM)
1750 E. Northrop Blvd., Suite 200
Chandler, AZ 85286-1744
phone: (800) 460-6276
website: www.nasm.org

The NASM offers certifications, continuing education, and tools for health and fitness and sports medicine professionals. It offers the certified personal trainer and other exercise certifications. The NASM also offers more than twenty continuing-education courses. The website includes training resources, exam prep workshops, and information about its certification programs.

National Strength and Conditioning Association (NSCA)
1885 Bob Johnson Dr.
Colorado Springs, CO 80906
phone: (800) 815-6826
website: www.nsca.com

The NSCA is a worldwide authority on strength and conditioning. The NSCA publishes the *Strength and Conditioning Journal* and the *Journal of Strength and Conditioning Research*. The website contains a free NSCA certification handbook, which explains how to become a certified fitness trainer, and information on events, grants, scholarships, and education courses.

Physical Education Teacher

What Does a Physical Education Teacher Do?

Mike Doyle is a physical education (PE) teacher at a Minnesota high school. He works with students who have physical and cognitive challenges. As an adaptive PE teacher, part of his job is to modify physical education activities to help his students participate and succeed in PE. When his students first see the ropes course (an obstacle course created using ropes), they do not think they can complete the challenging activity. Doyle cheers them on and motivates them step-by-step until everyone completes the course.

Doyle is one of thousands of PE teachers working in schools nationwide. Whether they are working with able-bodied students, students with disabilities, or top athletes, PE teachers help students embrace a healthy lifestyle through exercise, nutrition, and good health practices. PE is not just about running laps or doing sit-ups anymore. Today's PE programs emphasize healthy habits. On the Gopher

At a Glance:
Physical Education Teacher

Minimum Educational Requirements
Bachelor's degree

Personal Qualities
Athletic; motivating

Certification and Licensing
Physical education teaching credential

Working Conditions
Mostly outdoors or in gyms and classrooms

Salary Range
About $26,820 to $108,450

Number of Jobs
As of 2014, approximately 167,000

Future Job Outlook
Average

Sport website, Chad Triolet, the 2014 National Physical Education Teacher of the Year, explains that "success-driven physical education is all about designing and implementing a student-centered program where ALL students have a chance to develop skills and concepts that will help them be lifelong movers who make healthy choices."

PE teachers follow local, state, and national health and fitness standards. Most states require PE teachers to prepare students to pass physical performance tests. Teachers prepare lesson plans containing the learning objective, preassessment, activities, location, student grouping, and evaluation methods. Teachers include modifications to meet class size, available equipment, and the needs of students with disabilities. They also motivate students to do their best. During an interview with the author, Jennifer Carlson, a middle school PE teacher, stressed the importance of making lessons meaningful: "I think that any time a teacher can make a lesson/concept more *personal/relevant* to a student's life, it will raise the 'motivation factor'

Students get a lesson on proper basketball techniques from their physical education teacher. PE teachers teach students rules, techniques, and sportsmanship—but they also try to help students develop skills for lifelong healthy living.

a lot! In PE that might mean relating a concept like balance, for example, to something outside school that a student enjoys (surfing, skating, etc.)." PE teachers provide positive feedback to improve students' skills. They also evaluate attitude and level of physical fitness, which is used to determine a student's grade.

In many states elementary PE is taught by the classroom teacher, but in some it is taught by a specialized PE teacher. Elementary PE emphasizes basic skills and teamwork through educational games, dance, gymnastics, and sports. The focus is for everyone to participate and have fun. Teachers alter the rules and the sizes of teams or equipment to increase student activity levels. For example, a teacher might have students play three-on-three soccer rather than organizing eleven players into a single game. Teachers may teach lessons on hand washing, hygiene, reading nutrition labels, eating healthy foods, and coping with bullies and stress.

PE programs in middle school, high school, and college focus on lifelong fitness activities like running, tennis, swimming, and weight training. In addition to helping students develop the skills needed for these activities, PE teachers give lessons in nutrition and health science and show students how to use heart rate monitors and other technology to achieve optimal exercise benefits. Many teachers have added technology to their classes. Music from students' iPods motivates them to raise their heart rates while exercising to their favorite songs. Flip cameras and other digital video devices enable students to record one another performing a PE task and then watch themselves to fine-tune their technique.

Many PE teachers also coach competitive school sports teams. They plan, organize, and teach skills and techniques to help teams win. They conduct team trainings, attend the competitions, and give encouragement and feedback during games. Coaching usually involves teaching students the importance of balancing athletic skill with academic achievement and overall fitness. Steve McLaughlin, a San Diego high school boys' volleyball coach, explained in an e-mail to the author how he motivates athletes: "Coaching the heart of an athlete is often times overlooked as the focus tends to be on skill training, however when your athlete knows you care about their success and development as a person then they will give you great effort and their motivation will stay high during practices and competitions."

How Do You Become a Physical Education Teacher?

Education

High school students interested in a career as a PE teacher should take classes in biology, chemistry, health science, physics, anatomy, and physiology so they understand how the body works. This is in addition to PE classes. Active participation in school sports is also good preparation for becoming a PE teacher. A bachelor's degree from an accredited university or college is required to become a teacher. A master's degree is required to teach at colleges and universities. Most PE teachers earn a bachelor's degree in health and physical education, nutrition science, or kinesiology. Typical college courses include biomechanics, exercise physiology, nutrition and wellness, kinesiology, sports psychology, and motor development as well as fitness activity classes like tennis.

The next step is to enter a teacher preparation program, which focuses on effective teaching and classroom management strategies. This usually involves a student-teaching or internship component where the student teacher works with an experienced teacher to learn and apply effective instructional strategies. Typical courses include methods of teaching games, adapted physical education, motor development, PE evaluation methods, and team sports.

Certification and Licensing

All fifty states, the District of Columbia, and Puerto Rico require public school teachers to be licensed. A teaching credential is a license granted to individuals who have met requirements mandated by their state board of education. Prospective PE teachers should contact their state department of education to verify the teacher certification requirements. Most states require passage of a basic skills test in reading, writing, and mathematics as well as a specialty exam demonstrating that they have mastered physical education skills. A background check is also required. Once all of the requirements have been met, the teacher will be issued an initial single-subject PE credential to teach kindergarten through twelfth (K–12) grades. This preliminary credential is valid for five years. Over the next five years, the teacher must complete additional credits for the preliminary credential to be cleared or completed. The clear teaching credential must be renewed every five years. Parochial and private schools may have their own certification requirements.

Volunteer Work and Internships

Aspiring PE teachers can gain valuable experience by volunteering for local community centers, youth sports organizations, and other groups. Volunteers may get to lead sports activities, giving them hands-on experience working with children. Local park and recreation centers offer sports volunteering opportunities, including fun runs, dance, gymnastics, and other athletic programs. Sports organizations like the American Youth Soccer Organization offer volunteer positions to students as young as age twelve. Duties may include lining and patrolling fields or assisting coaches.

Many youth sports organizations pay volunteers to coach and referee after the student completes a training course. Include Autism, a San Diego–based nonprofit program for kids and teens diagnosed with an autism spectrum disorder, organizes inclusion baseball games in which peer volunteers ages twelve to twenty-two lead autistic players on the field, help them follow the rules, and enjoy the game of baseball. According to Jake, a seventeen-year-old student in San Diego, volunteering can be very rewarding. "By volunteering with Include Autism's Inclusion Baseball League," Jake says in an e-mail to the author, "I have made many new friends and learned the importance of perseverance. Watching the kids grow as players and as people is truly an amazing experience to be a part of!"

Skills and Personality

Like all educators, PE teachers should be skilled in their subject area, counsels the National Board for Professional Teaching Standards. For PE teachers, this includes sports, fitness, diet, nutrition, and wellness. Paul Rosenguard, the former executive director of Sports Play and Active Recreation for Kids and also a former PE teacher, stated in an e-mail to the author, "I'm a believer that if you teach physical education, you should be a role model, and that means being fit and living the lifestyle you advocate." PE teachers need to be physically fit and skilled so that they can demonstrate the techniques required for games, sports, and fitness activities. Students are more likely to eat nutritious foods and make healthy life choices if their teacher models making healthy food and lifestyle choices.

PE teachers motivate students to achieve their personal best. They must have a positive attitude to support and cheer students for their individual progress toward goals. Having a love of sports, passion for teaching, and a strong desire to help children all contribute to being able to motivate students to have fun exercising and learn healthy life habits.

Physical education teachers must also possess exceptional communications skills. They describe the rules of games and sports to students by breaking down complex concepts and instructions into smaller, understandable ideas. They provide students with constructive feedback that encourages them to improve.

On the Job

Employers

PE teachers are employed by preschools; elementary, middle, and high schools; and universities—both public and private. During the two-month summer vacation, many PE teachers work a second job teaching health, fitness, or sports at summer camps.

Working Conditions

The perks of being a PE teacher are wearing comfortable clothes and being able to work outside when the weather is nice. PE teachers have more flexible working conditions than other teachers and can utilize outdoor areas, indoor gyms, and even classroom settings. While the average teacher workday is seven hours, PE teachers who coach often work an average of eleven hours a day. In secondary schools, PE teachers usually work multiple periods a day and may have forty or more students per period. Elementary PE teachers often work in more than one school and must factor travel time between schools into their schedules.

Earnings

Salaries vary by state and school district. The Bureau of Labor Statistics (BLS) shows that the average salary of a PE teacher is $63,770. According to career website Sokanu.com, salaries start from $26,820 and go up to $108,450. Many PE teachers at the middle and high school level earn additional stipends or money by coaching a sport. Sometimes the extra pay compensates them for the additional coaching hours; sometimes it does not. One recent study showed that about 20 percent of high school basketball and football coaches earned a stipend of at least $10,000 a year. But this is not necessarily the case for other sports.

Teachers also receive benefits such as health insurance and paid sick leave. Because they may not work for a couple months during the summer, they must budget their salary to cover the months they are not paid.

Opportunities for Advancement

PE teachers can advance their careers through experience and additional education. In addition to pay increases based on years of teaching, some PE teachers move on to administrative posts such as PE directors, adapted PE specialists, or athletic directors. Many middle and high school PE teachers advance their careers by becoming assistant coaches or coaches.

What Is the Future Outlook for Physical Education Teachers?

There are approximately 167,000 PE teachers in the United States. The BLS predicts that the PE teacher job market will grow 12.2 percent through 2022. California, Texas, and New York offer the greatest job prospects. Job opportunities are influenced by state budgets, student enrollment, and the number of job applicants. According to the article "Health Concerns Spark Demand for Physical Education Teachers" on the College Foundation of North Carolina website, "Many hope that changes in public perception towards physical education will spark a demand for more physical education teachers."

Find Out More

PE Central
website: www.pecentral.org

This website for K–12 PE teachers offers over two thousand PE lesson ideas, assessments, and best practices and over one hundred physical activity–related videos. PE Central also offers a series of programs designed to motivate children to improve their fitness and activity.

PEteacherEDU.org
website: www.peteacheredu.org

PEteacherEDU.org is a website developed to help aspiring PE teachers understand the steps required to become certified educators. This comprehensive resource includes links to each state's PE teacher certification requirements, careers, salaries, and PE resources.

SHAPE America—Society of Health and Physical Educators
1900 Association Dr.
Reston, VA 20191
phone: (800) 213-7193
website: www.shapeamerica.org

As the nation's largest membership organization of health and physical education professionals, SHAPE America works with its fifty state affiliates and national partners to support Let's Move!, Presidential Youth Fitness Program, Active Schools, and the Jump Rope for Heart/Hoops for Heart programs. Its website contains extensive information about how to become a PE teacher.

Sports Play and Active Recreation for Kids (SPARK)
438 Camino Del Rio South, Suite 110
San Diego, CA 92108
e-mail: spark@sparkpe.org
website: www.sparkpe.org

This organization is dedicated to creating, implementing, and evaluating programs that promote lifelong wellness. This site includes links to resources, grants, related organizations, and sample PE lessons.

Recreational Therapist

What Does a Recreational Therapist Do?

When four-year-old Alex had a spinal cord injury, he lost function in his legs and had to use a wheelchair for mobility. Melissa Pavlowsky, a certified therapeutic recreational specialist (CTRS) at the Children's Institute in Pittsburgh, Pennsylvania, helped him learn to cope with his injury. She took him on community outings to practice his wheelchair skills outdoors, invited his cousins to play adapted sports (modified so disabled players can participate) with him, and encouraged him to join a wheelchair baseball team. She also connected his mother to various community resources, which led to Alex's participation in wheelchair baseball, sled hockey, and other activities.

Pavlowsky is one of thousands of recreational therapists (RTs) who design, direct, and coordinate recreation-based treatment programs to help patients manage or recover from a range of illnesses and injuries. RTs provide rehabilitation services to improve the client's independence and help him or her resume leisure

At a Glance:
Recreational Therapist

Minimum Educational Requirements
Bachelor's degree

Personal Qualities
Compassionate; flexible

Certification and Licensing
Required at medical facilities

Working Conditions
Indoors and outdoors

Salary Range
About $27,150 to $69,230

Number of Jobs
As of 2014, about 17,950

Future Job Outlook
Average

and social activities impacted by injury, illness, or addiction. They use arts, crafts, games, sports, music, and other therapy tools to maintain or enhance the client's cognitive, physical, emotional, and social health. These leisure activities help participants build strength and mobility, improve fine motor skills, boost self-confidence, make friends, and learn how to interact in the community.

RTs work with people of all ages and with all different physical and mental challenges. RTs generally work in physical medicine/rehabilitation, behavioral health (mental health and substance abuse clients), community inclusion services (helping injured or disabled clients become independent in their community), or with geriatric patients or patients with developmental disabilities. A typical day begins with an RT responding to a physician's orders for assessment and treatment. The therapist starts by reviewing the patient's current medical condition; assessing the client's physical, social, cognitive, and emotional needs; and identifying the client's favorite leisure activities. Using this information, the therapist creates a recreation plan to meet the patient's needs. Therapists provide both individual and group-based activities.

Recreational therapists use a variety of therapies to help patients. Some therapies involve art, music, dance, and movement. Others involve working with animals or plants, writing, or sports. For instance, an RT might use music, dance, and drama therapy to increase cognitive function, stimulate social interaction, and promote mental health in Alzheimer's patients.

Activity is a central feature of recreational therapy. Therapists might lead clients with mental illness, addictions, physical disabilities, or developmental disabilities on field trips to help them integrate into their communities. On a trip to the mall, therapists help clients in wheelchairs learn the mechanics of propelling a wheelchair over different surfaces, in and out of elevators, and through a line to order lunch. Taking developmentally disabled clients bowling helps them practice daily living skills like handling money, communicating with others, and following directions as well as getting exercise and socializing with peers. Treatment plans for injured veterans might focus on overcoming both psychological and physical trauma through activities like bowling to condition muscles, foster camaraderie, and build a support network. According to the American Therapeutic Recreation Association (ATRA) website, "Research supports the concept that people with active, satisfying lifestyles will be happier and healthier."

Therapists also teach patients strategies to help them cope with their disability or illness so they can enjoy social and recreational activities. For example, clients with spinal cord injuries often need help learning how to cope with the emotions of being in a wheelchair. In an interview with the author, Pavlowsky explains how she helps clients work through emotional barriers: "Many clients struggle emotionally with being in a wheelchair. As an RT, I can really focus on the person themselves and what they are feeling. When on an outing, I use talk therapy to help them deal with their emotions and to advocate for themselves." Pavlowsky also helps her clients find polite but firm ways to respond to strangers who ask intrusive questions or offer unwanted help.

How Do You Become a Recreational Therapist?

Education

A bachelor's degree in recreational therapy or a related field is the minimum educational requirement to become a certified therapist and usually requires four years to complete. Those who earn a two-year associate's degree are qualified for entry-level positions in the recreational therapy field. Most recreational therapy programs feature various specialized classes (in clinical practice and assessment, for instance) as well as more general classes in recreational therapy, human anatomy, and psychology. Bachelor's programs include fieldwork where students obtain valuable hands-on experience working with patients in an internship under the supervision of a certified RT.

Certification

Although many employers, especially medical facilities, prefer to hire a CTRS, as of 2015 only California and Washington require all RTs to be certified. New Hampshire, North Carolina, Oklahoma, and

Utah require RTs to be licensed. The National Council for Therapeutic Recreation Certification (NCTRC) reports that more than twelve thousand RTs are certified by its organization.

Certification requirements include completing a bachelor's degree or higher from an accredited university, participating in a supervised internship of at least 560 hours, and passing a national certification examination. Every five years the therapist must renew the certification by accumulating continuing-education classes, gaining work experience, and/or retesting. Specialty certifications in behavioral health, community inclusion services, developmental disabilities, geriatrics, and physical medicine/rehabilitation are also offered by the NCTRC. Other organizations grant certification for specific therapy techniques, such as aquatic therapy, equine therapy, or aromatherapy, which qualifies RTs to use these therapies with patients.

Volunteer Work and Internships

Students who are interested in recreational therapy can gain valuable experience by volunteering at park and recreation centers, senior centers, hospitals, or with the Special Olympics and other community organizations that serve the disabled population. For example, Montgomery County Recreation in Maryland recruits teenage volunteers to assist with programs for disabled youth. These include helping with classes and special events, serving as companions, and working at summer camps. Applicants must be at least fourteen, able to commit to the length of the program, provide three references, and demonstrate enthusiasm for recreational activities.

The ATRA website has an internship database listing over one hundred internships. The Bend Park and Recreation District in Bend, Oregon, provides fourteen- to sixteen-week undergraduate and graduate internships that give interns hands-on practice working with clients who have a wide range of physical and intellectual disabilities. Interns participate in a variety of activities, such as adapted skiing, kayaking, rafting, creative arts, and exploring nature.

Skills and Personality

Compassion and empathy are key personality traits for RTs. They should be caring, gentle, and sympathetic when working with patients and their families. Patients who are disabled, elderly, in pain, or ill benefit from therapists who are professional and patient. These clients often require extra time and special attention.

RTs utilize play therapy and other recreational therapies, so they should be creative, upbeat, and fun-loving people. Their enthusiasm encourages clients to participate to the best of their abilities and may coax depressed or disabled individuals to try new activities.

RTs must be flexible. They must be able to create, develop, and implement intervention programs for each client. Often they quickly think of ways to adapt activities to accommodate each patient's abilities and disabilities. Clients with physical disabilities may require modified equipment to enable them to participate in activities. For example, some RTs use softballs that beep and basketballs that jingle to enable blind clients to play softball and basketball.

Strong communication skills are also an important part of this job. Effective RTs possess both strong listening and speaking skills. They listen to a patient's problems, concerns, and interests and then use this information to create an effective course of treatment or therapy program designed for that patient. They give clear directions during activities, explain treatment programs and community resources, and give instructions on effective coping strategies.

On the Job

Employers

RTs work in a variety of public and private settings. The BLS reports that 35 percent work in local, state, and private hospitals. RTs also work in nursing and residential care facilities, substance abuse centers, rehabilitation centers, special education departments, and park and recreation departments. State and federal agencies such as the Department of Veterans Affairs also employ RTs.

Working Conditions

RTs work in a variety of settings. They might spend part of their day in an office attending meetings, planning activities, writing patient assessment reports, or performing other administrative duties. They might also travel to provide direct services to the client. Therapists may meet with clients in hospitals or other facilities, in clients' homes, or in the community. For example, they may help clients master daily living skills such as riding a bus or going to a grocery store. Some therapists and their patients travel to parks and recreation areas to practice sports and outdoor activities like fishing, baseball, or hiking.

According to the US Department of Labor, three-fourths of RTs work full time. Some therapists work evenings and weekends to meet clients' needs. During the workday, they spend a lot of time on their feet. Sometimes they physically assist patients or lift heavy objects like wheelchairs. They must practice safe lifting techniques to prevent work-related injuries.

Earnings

The BLS reports that salaries for RTs range from $27,150 to $69,230. Education, work experience, work setting, and job location all influence salary. According to TherapistSchools.com, education is the key to higher salaries for RTs: "The most well paid recreational therapists are the most highly educated ones." The BLS reports that the top-paying industries for RTs are federal, state, and local governments, $65,540; home health care services, $50,320; specialty hospitals, $49,520; and general medical and surgical hospitals, $49,520. It also reports that the highest annual wages for RTs are offered in California, $59,730; Connecticut, $54,780; New Jersey, $54,010; New York, $51,260; and the District of Columbia, $50,600.

Opportunities for Advancement

The opportunities for advancement in this field are better for those who obtain a bachelor's degree, several years of work experience, or specialized certificates. RTs can advance to administrative or managerial roles in hospitals, rehabilitation centers, park and recreation centers, and other health care centers. Therapists who earn a doctorate degree can apply to teach at the university level.

What Is the Future Outlook for Recreational Therapists?

The BLS predicts that employment of RTs will grow 13 percent through 2022, which is the average for all occupations. RTs with a bachelor's degree and certification will have the best job prospects. Therapists who earn certification in geriatric therapy should have the greatest employment opportunities. As members of the baby-boom generation age, they are expected to require recreational therapy to treat Alzheimer's disease, strokes, and other age-related injuries and illnesses. RTs also will be needed to help healthy seniors remain active and independent. In addition, these therapists will be needed to teach the growing number of people with chronic conditions like diabetes and obesity how to manage their conditions and maintain their mobility. Increased legislation requiring federally funded services for disabled students will increase the need for these therapists in educational settings.

Find Out More

American Therapeutic Recreation Association (ATRA)
629 N. Main St.
Hattiesburg, MS 39401
phone: (601) 450-2872
website: www.atra-online.com

ATRA is the largest national organization serving the interests and needs of CTRSs and RTs in the United States. The website includes links to education, networking, policy and legislation, resources, a bookstore, and job and internship opportunities.

Commission on Accreditation of Allied Health Education Programs
1361 Park St.
Clearwater, FL 33756
phone: (727) 210-2350
website: www.caahep.org

The commission is a postsecondary accrediting agency providing information on health careers. It accredits more than twenty-one hundred entry-level education programs in twenty-eight health science professions. Its website includes the educational, curriculum, credentialing, licensing, and certification requirements for RTs. It also has links to career-planning publications.

National Council for Therapeutic Recreation Certification (NCTRC)
7 Elmwood Dr.
New City, NY 10956
phone: (845) 639-1439
website: www.nctrc.org

NCTRC is a nonprofit international organization devoted to ensuring professional quality through the certification of RTs. The NCTRC grants the CTRS credential to therapists who meet high standards for certification, including education, work experience, and continuing professional development. The website includes recent news, standards and publications, links to other resources, and frequently asked questions.

National Therapeutic Recreation Society (NTRS)
22377 Belmont Ridge Rd.
Ashburn, VA 20148
phone: (703) 858-0784
website: www.recreationtherapy.com/history/ntrs/ntrs2005archive.htm

NTRS is part of the National Recreation and Park Association. The society specializes in providing therapeutic recreation services for individuals with disabilities in both clinical facilities and the community. Its website contains information on education and training, leadership, programs, publications, reports, resources, and legislative updates.

Therapeutic Recreation Directory
website: www.recreationtherapy.com

This independent recreational therapy website contains information and resources on recreational therapy, creative arts, in-home recreation, physical education for special populations, music therapy, equestrian therapy, and related therapies. It includes links to colleges offering therapeutic recreation programs, and organizations at the international, national, and state levels.

Recreation Worker

Sean Provencio is a camp counselor success story. Like many sixteen- and seventeen-year-olds, he didn't know what his purpose was. A counselor at YMCA Camp Marston in Julian, California, changed all of that by creating a positive environment that unlocked his potential. In an e-mail to the author, Provencio explained, "From a lost teen to a goal-oriented young adult, I can truly say going to camp and continuing to work around kids has opened my view to new approaches on almost everything." Provencio is now a summer camp counselor and works with children in an after-school program.

Provencio is one of thousands of mostly young men and women who plan and lead leisure activities for groups in volunteer organizations or recreation facilities, including aquatic centers, camps, parks, playgrounds, and senior centers. They direct activities like arts and crafts, camping, sports, adventure programs, and music. From "Mommy/Daddy

At a Glance:
Recreation Worker

Minimum Educational Requirements

High school diploma for some jobs; bachelor's degree for others

Personal Qualities

Physically fit; excellent communication skills

Certification and Licensing

Varies by state

Working Conditions

Indoors and outdoors

Salary Range

For low-level positions, about $17,000 to $39,000; for high-level positions such as parks and recreation director, about $31,000 to $101,000

Number of Jobs

As of 2012, about 345,400

Future Job Outlook

Average

and Me" classes for toddlers to an after-school chess club for elementary schoolchildren, to ballroom dance classes for seniors, recreation workers provide services to clients of all ages.

A recreation worker's job is not all fun and games, though. These personnel also explain and enforce safety rules and regulations to prevent injury and maintain discipline. They administer basic first aid and call emergency medical assistance if needed. Greeting new arrivals, answering questions about programs, and encouraging participation are routine duties. They supervise the daily operations of recreational facilities, including answering phones, registering new clients, and maintaining equipment.

Recreation workers have many different job titles, and their duties differ greatly according to their job assignment, education, work experience, and certification. The four most common jobs are camp counselors, camp directors, activity specialists, and parks and recreation directors. Camp counselors work with youth in overnight or day camps. They instruct children and teens in outdoor activities, which may include hiking, horseback riding, arts and crafts, swimming, and canoeing. Some counselors teach specialized courses like archery, sailing, drama, and music. Theo Meyers, a camp counselor in San Diego, says the emphasis is on enjoyment. Meyers commented in an e-mail to the author, "Always remember to have fun. The whole point of recreation is to create smiles."

Counselors provide guidance and emotional support, encourage socialization, and supervise daily camp life. These counselors teach youth about the environment and encourage an understanding and appreciation of nature. Camp counselors keep campers safe by explaining and enforcing safety rules. Camp directors perform administrative duties to keep the camp running smoothly. They supervise camp counselors and other employees, plan camp events or activities, hold fundraising events, place advertising, and participate in public relations and community outreach. Balancing the budget, paying the bills, hiring staff, and recruiting volunteers are all important parts of this job.

Activity specialists provide instruction in one activity, like dance, swimming, or tennis. They work in a variety of settings, including cruise ships, camps, aquatic centers, parks and recreation centers, senior centers, and after-school programs. They plan lessons to meet the ability level of each group, instruct, motivate, and monitor participants. Unlike camp counselors who are generally assigned one group of children or teens, the activity specialist teaches multiple groups of students each workday.

Parks and recreation directors create and supervise comprehensive recreation programs in parks, playgrounds, aquatic centers, senior centers, and other community centers. These programs include sports, enrichment classes, and community events. For example, San Diego's Park and Recreation Department features a dance arts program, senior citizen services, sports activities, and therapeutic recreation services for disabled citizens. Its director oversees the budget and staff to make sure each program is a success. The director creates an annual budget, which must be approved by the city council. Hiring, training, and managing staff and volunteers are critical parts of the job. These directors also supervise revenue earned by the parks and recreation department. Revenue sources include park entrance fees, facility rentals, and registration fees for classes. For example, rental fees are charged for renting pavilions for parties, and sports leagues pay to reserve the city's fields for their games. Ultimately, the success of a community's parks and recreation program depends on its director.

How Do You Become a Recreation Worker?

Education

To prepare for a career as a recreation worker, high school students should take classes in arts and crafts, music, dance, drama, athletics, and nature study. Some part-time or seasonal recreation jobs require only a high school diploma and provide on-the-job training. Full-time positions generally require a bachelor's degree with a major in parks and recreation, leisure studies, or public administration—all of which usually take four years to complete. As of 2012, eighty-one bachelor's degree programs in recreation or leisure studies were accredited by the Council on Accreditation of Parks, Recreation, Tourism, and Related Professions. Courses in these programs usually include community organization, management, supervision, administration, and human development. In addition, students take classes preparing them to work with the elderly or disabled. Some students specialize in park management, outdoor recreation, industrial or commercial recreation, or camp management.

Certification and Licensing

Certification and licensing depend on the job requirements and vary from state to state. For example, most states require swim instructors to be certified. The National Recreation and Park Association (NRPA) is the primary certifying agency in this field and qualifies individuals for many professional and technical jobs. NRPA grants the certified park and recreation professional (CPRP) designation to recreation workers who pass a national examination; earn a bachelor's degree with a major in recreation, park resources, or leisure services from an accredited program; and have a minimum of five years of full-time work experience. The NRPA currently administers four certification programs: the CPRP, the certified park and recreation executive, the certified playground safety inspector, and the aquatic facility operator. To maintain certification, workers must meet continuing-education requirements every two years.

Volunteer Work and Internships

There are many volunteer opportunities in the recreation field. Many teenagers work as activity leaders at after-school programs and in youth organizations, camps, hospitals, nursing homes, and senior centers. Students interested in volunteering in the recreation field should contact local parks and recreation departments, nursing and personal care facilities, or local social or religious organizations.

Many parks and recreation departments offer internships in a variety of departments. Interested individuals are advised to contact the internship coordinator at the local parks and recreation facility. For example, on the website of the Portland Parks & Recreation (PP&R) department, the following internship job description is listed: "Assist in the development and facilitation of programs and activities at the various PP&R community centers. Work directly with program coordinators, center directors, community members, families, and students."

According to the American Camp Association, many camps offer summer internships for undergraduates and graduates. In some cases, these internships are affiliated with a college or university, and interns may be able to earn a stipend and/or college credit. At Camp Towanda in Homesdale, Pennsylvania, for example, interns get paid and also get free room and board. But most of all, the camp's website explains, "you get to make a real difference in children's lives while learning real-world career-building skills."

Skills and Personality

Recreation workers must be physically fit. Their job requires them to be on their feet for long periods of time as they demonstrate activities, move among participants, and carry equipment and materials. Recreation workers may spend long hours in the pool, at camp, or in the sun.

They must also be flexible when planning and monitoring activities. They use problem-solving skills to alter plans when equipment, facilities, or weather conditions change. Whether helping a reluctant child with separation anxiety, coaxing a disabled client to try a new activity, or finding a solution for an upset parent, maintaining a calm, courteous, and professional manner is a vital skill for this profession.

Recreation workers must have good communication skills; they often work with large groups and must be able to give clear directions, encourage and motivate participants, and enforce order and safety rules. Because their clients are often children, disabled, or elderly, they must be able to modify their instructions to meet the age and needs of these clients.

On the Job

Employers

Recreation workers are employed in a variety of settings, including summer camps, cruise ships, parks, community centers, theme parks, and playgrounds. They also work in residential care facilities, nursing homes, and community and vocational rehabilitation centers. According to the Bureau of Labor Statistics (BLS), approximately half of the full-time recreation workers are employed by city and county government parks and recreation departments. About 20 percent work for youth organizations, including the YMCA, the Boys & Girls Clubs, scouting associations, and other child-focused groups.

Working Conditions

Working conditions depend upon the job description and activities, but many recreation workers spend part of their day working outside in a variety of weather conditions. Although some recreation workers hold full-time jobs, many of these jobs are part time, seasonal, and temporary. Irregular hours, including working nights and weekends, are not uncommon because many activities are scheduled for times when children are out of school and adults are off work. Workers who become recreation directors and supervisors are more likely to work in an office, spending less time working with clients and more time planning special events and programs.

Earnings

According to the BLS, the annual salary range for camp counselors, camp directors, and activity specialists varies from $17,190 to $39,230, depending upon the job description and location as well as the worker's experience, education, and certification. The average salary for recreation workers is $22,240. Average wages are highest in the District of Columbia, $45,880; Nevada, $34,530; Hawaii, $33,560; Vermont, $32,700; and Connecticut, $30,740.

Because their job has more challenging responsibilities and higher education requirements, parks and recreation directors earn higher salaries. The website Salary.com reports that parks and recreation directors earn $30,802 to $101,020. Director salaries are based on the size of the camp or city and the number of employees. Larger cities and camps generate larger income, translating into larger salaries for the directors.

Opportunities for Advancement

Recreation workers can move up the career ladder in this field by furthering their education and gaining job experience. With an additional two years of study, recreation workers can earn a master's degree in parks and recreation, business administration, or public administration, enabling them to assume supervisory positions. A doctorate degree in this field requires two more years and prepares the worker for higher-level administrative positions or teaching positions at the college and university levels.

What Is the Future Outlook for Recreation Workers?

The BLS predicts that employment for recreation workers will grow 14 percent through 2022, which will add 82,500 new positions. The best job prospects will be for employees seeking part-time or seasonal recreation employment. The projected job increase is due to growing demand for recreational activities for older adults and people with special needs. The rise in childhood obesity has motivated many state and federal agencies to promote healthy activities for children, which will generate more recreation worker jobs. These factors will spur job growth in senior centers, halfway houses, camps, sports clinics, swimming pools, and daycare programs for people with special needs.

Find Out More

American Academy for Park & Recreation Administration (AAPRA)
PO Box 888
Mahomet, IL 61853
phone: (217) 590-0231
e-mail: info@aapra.org
website: www.aapra.org

The AAPRA is an organization of high-level parks and recreation administrators with at least fifteen years of experience or who manage parks and recreation departments with populations over fifty thousand. Its website has links to awards, scholarships, a journal, mentorship opportunities, and member videos.

American Camp Association (ACA)
5000 State Rd. 67 North
Martinsville, IN 46151-7902
phone: (800) 428-2267
website: www.acacamps.org

For over one hundred years the ACA and its community of camp professionals have worked to share their knowledge and expertise to ensure the quality of camp programs. Its website offers a wealth of information to preserve, promote, and improve the camp experience. Website links include ways to get involved, news, education and events, publications and research, and jobs.

National Recreation and Park Association (NRPA)
22377 Belmont Ridge Rd.
Ashburn, VA 20148
phone: (800) 626-NRPA
website: www.nrpa.org

The NRPA is the largest nonprofit organization devoted to promoting public parks, recreation, and conservation. Its website offers professional development, research, certification information, and volunteer and internship opportunities. Resources include NPRA's Success Story Database, the *Parks & Recreation* magazine, and an online question-and-answer feature.

YMCA of the USA
101 N. Wacker Dr.
Chicago, IL 60606
website: www.ymca.net

The YMCA is an international organization focused on nurturing the potential of children, encouraging people to live healthier lives, and strengthening communities. Its website has links to leadership camps, which help students develop skills to become recreation workers. YMCAs offer volunteer opportunities to give aspiring recreation workers valuable hands-on experiences.

Sports Dietitian

When a sixteen-year-old female runner felt like she was having a heart attack and called 911, her doctor ruled out heart trouble and referred her to Barbara Lewin, a certified specialist in sports dietetics (CSSD). Lewin discovered that the high school track star was trying to lose weight by using energy drinks, skipping meals, and taking two weight-loss supplements. Lewin showed the girl that her diet contained three stimulants: caffeine, ephedra, and guarana. She worked with the runner to create a healthy and safe weight-loss program.

Sports dietitians like Lewin provide individual and group nutrition counseling to help athletes understand their nutritional needs and devise healthy diets as a means to improve athletic performance. Sports dietitians work with clients of all ages and abilities, including professional and recreational athletes and the military. They may work with one individual or a high school, college, Olympic, or professional sports team. In a phone interview, Lewin related, "I've given nutrition advice to clients from tennis stars and ultra-endurance athletes to an

At a Glance:
Sports Dietitian

Minimum Educational Requirements
Bachelor's degree

Personal Qualities
Excellent communication skills; analytical

Certification and Licensing
State license varies by state

Working Conditions
Indoors and outdoors

Salary Range
About $42,000 to $90,000

Number of Jobs
As of 2012, about 67,400

Future Job Outlook
Better than average

eighty-seven-year-old who wanted to climb Mount Kilimanjaro for her bucket list." Dietitians also may work with clients with medical issues such as eating disorders, obesity, and diabetes. Some sports dietitians educate older patients on diet and nutrition to slow aging as well as the loss of bone and muscle mass. While the terms *dietitian* and *nutritionist* are often used interchangeably, only registered dietitians have completed the educational requirements to obtain certification by the Commission on Dietetic Registration (CDR).

When sports dietitians first meet with a client, they conduct an intake interview to assess the individual's health, needs, and diet. They identify the client's goals, food likes and dislikes, food allergies, and dietary practices. They may also assess body composition and energy balance (intake versus expenditure). Sports dietitians analyze this data to determine the individual's current performance and health and to set attainable performance goals.

Taking into account the latest sports nutrition research, sports dietitians create a nutrition plan tailored to each client. Because athletes have different nutritional needs during different exercise phases, the plan should provide optimal nutrition recommendations for training, competing, and recovery. The plan includes what foods to eat and what not to eat, supplements to use and those to avoid, and the amounts of protein and carbohydrates for each meal. In an interview with the author, Lewin reported that she often counsels athletes about the dangers of supplements: "The supplement industry is a multimillion-dollar industry that targets athletes. Supplements are not well regulated, and there are many that can cause more harm than good." Other nutrition recommendations may address hydration, illness prevention, weight management, and eating disorders. The nutrition plan includes individualized meals and snacks to support the athlete's body mass, body fat, and muscle mass goals and to enhance health and athletic performance goals. Once the athlete begins using the plan, the dietician monitors performance and health over a period of time to determine if adjustments are needed.

Some sports dietitians also work in hospitals, clinics, and rehabilitation centers. These specialized dietitians coordinate nutritional therapy with a medical team, which may include sports medicine physicians, physical therapists, and nurses. For example, they may use nutrition therapy to manage medical conditions or to speed recovery from a sports injury or illness. In cardiac rehabilitation centers, they counsel patients who have suffered a heart attack or who have had surgery about healthy eating habits. They may also work with patients with disordered eating to help follow a nutritious food plan.

Sports dietitians often work as independent consultants. They are often hired by groups, companies, and health/wellness centers to promote better nutrition in the community by giving lectures about diet, nutrition, supplements, and how healthy eating habits prevent or manage many diseases like diabetes. Some also present sports nutrition education for health/wellness programs. Because nutrition research is constantly changing, sports dietitians must continually keep up with the newest nutritional science research to maintain high professional standards.

How Do You Become a Sports Dietitian?

Education

High school students who have an interest in becoming a sports dietician should take courses in life sciences, chemistry, biochemistry, food science, math and statistics, health, psychology, and physical education. A bachelor's degree, which usually takes four years, is an essential starting point to becoming a sports dietitian. Many universities have departments in nutrition and exercise science/physiology or kinesiology. College-level coursework includes the study of food and nutrition sciences, food service systems management, business, biochemistry, and other science classes. Many programs include internships where students apply what they have learned in the academic program to real-life situations. Interns work in medical and sports settings to gain hands-on experience under the supervision of a certified sports dietitian. According to the Bureau of Labor Statistics (BLS), the majority of sports dietitians have advanced degrees, which make them more competitive in the job market. A master's degree requires an additional one to two years of study. Those with a doctoral degree will qualify for job opportunities in education, research, management, and administration.

Certification and Licensing

The CDR is the credentialing agency for the Academy of Nutrition and Dietetics (AND). It reports that forty-six states require dietitians to be licensed. Requirements and regulations vary from state to state and include a wide selection of certification types, so aspiring dietitians should consult their state's regulatory board for up-to-date information. According to the CDR, to become certified, candidates must be registered dietitians with documentation of fifteen hundred hours of specialty experience within five years. To maintain certification, they must document another one thousand hours of specialty experience within the next five years.

Volunteer Work and Internships

Volunteering for a youth sport group, YMCA or other youth organization, high school or college team, or a local running or biking group will help aspiring sports dietitians learn the mental, physical, and nutritional demands of a sport. Shadowing a sports dietitian in a medical or sports setting will provide insight into the daily duties, resources, and latest sports research findings and gives hands-on experience with hydration and fueling strategies to help teams during training, travel, and competitions.

Skills and Personality

Flexibility and adaptability are key personality traits for sports dietitians. This is especially true for those who work with elite athletes or with athletes at higher competitive levels. These athletes often have rigorous training, practice, and competition schedules that might conflict with dietary needs and plans. In an article on the website of *Today's Dietitian* magazine, Nanna Meyer, a senior sports dietitian with the US Olympic Committee, explains the importance of being flexible when working with athletes at this level. "A lot of our work needs to be very flexible," Meyer says. "If you come into the [training] camp with a plan, you'll realize quickly that it probably won't work out the way you want. Thus, I would say the biggest challenge is related to the ever-changing schedule around the athletes' training and competing."

Sports dietitians must also possess analytical skills and an aptitude for science. They read, research, and interpret the latest scientific findings. It is vital that they understand the research well enough that they can apply it to their clients' food plans and are able to explain the research in terms the athlete, parent, coach, and others can understand. The ability to separate truth from fiction in claims about dietary supplements and other sports nutrition aids is also a valuable analytical skill for a sports dietitian.

Strong listening, speaking, and writing skills are also important for this career. A sports dietitian should listen to a client's current eating habits without judgment so that he or she feels comfortable being honest. A sports dietitian gets new clients by "selling" his or her services. As Lewin explains, "At some point in your career you will have to get up in front of a sports team to make a presentation to be hired." To develop this skill, she recommends students take speech classes or join Toastmasters, an organization that teaches public speaking. Sports dietitians must have excellent writing skills, because they often create written dietary plans and keep written records to track clients' progress.

On the Job

Employers

According to the BLS, 11 percent of all dietitians are self-employed and work as consultants on a contractual basis. It further reports that 31 percent work for local, state, or private hospitals. Sports dietitians are employed by universities, professional sports organizations, food corporations, fitness clubs, schools, cafeterias, nursing homes, and corporate wellness programs. They also find employment in medical settings such as cardiac rehabilitation, family practice offices, and with physicians specializing in bariatric surgery (weight-loss surgery performed on the stomach or intestines).

Working Conditions

Sports dietitians who work in medical settings often have a traditional five-day, forty-hour week. However, self-employed dietitians and those who work for sports teams often travel, work long hours, and work evenings and weekends to accommodate clients' schedules. On the website *Today's Dietitian*, Meyer further explains the complexities of traveling with the Olympic team: "While traveling around the world is easy to romanticize, the reality is that when these dietitians are out in the field, they're working 15-hour days and experiencing ever-changing situations."

Earnings

According to the Newswise website, beginning registered sports dietitians earn around $42,000. Full-time registered sports dietitians earn an average salary of about $75,050. Those with additional experience and education earn close to $90,000. Those with credentials in nutrition as well as strength and conditioning or athletic training earn salaries above $100,000. Salaries are based on the certifications, experience, the employer, and the location of employment. Per the website NutritionED.org, the annual average salaries are highest in California, $71,870; Nevada, $70,058; Hawaii, $64,150; Maryland, $64,120; and Connecticut, $63,820. Those employed full time generally receive a benefit package including health insurance, paid vacation, sick days, and retirement benefits.

Opportunities for Advancement

Sports dietitians may advance their careers through higher education, advanced nutrition certifications, and by gaining extensive experience to become consultants, lecturers, teachers, or self-employed business owners. Earning an advanced degree enables sports dietitians to advance to administration, research, or collegiate education positions. As sports dietitians gain experience working with athletes, they may advance from working with high school teams to working with college, professional, or Olympic sports teams. Famous athletes are more likely to hire the most educated and experienced sports dietitians.

What Is the Future Outlook for Sports Dietitians?

Dietitians, in general, can expect job opportunities to increase by more than 21 percent through 2022. The BLS predicts that there will be 14,200 new openings for all dietitians and nutritionists. According to the *US News & World Report* website, sports dietitian jobs will grow because of continuing concern about health, weight, and diet: "The growing number of health-conscious parents, as well as increased national attention on the heightened numbers of obese Americans and skyrocketing health care costs should keep this profession growing."

Find Out More

Commission on Dietetic Registration (CDR)
120 S. Riverside Plaza, Suite 2000
Chicago, IL 60606-6995
phone: (800) 877-1600
e-mail: cdr@eatright.org
website: www.cdrnet.org

The CDR administers the credentialing processes for dietitians wishing to become certified specialists in sports dietetics. Its website contains extensive information on the certification process as well as many resources for aspiring dietitians and those seeking nutrition counseling.

International Society of Sports Nutrition (ISSN)
4511 NW Seventh St.
Deerfield Beach, FL 33442
phone: (561) 239-1754
e-mail: issn.sports.nutrition@gmail.com
website: www.sportsnutritionsociety.org

The ISSN is the only not-for-profit academic-based association devoted to sports nutrition and the science of applied nutrition. Although most of the website's services are reserved for members, it does have links to certification study guides, information on how to become an ISSN-certified sports nutritionist, a newsletter, sports insider articles, and a Facebook page.

National Association of Sports Nutrition (NASN)
7710 Balboa Ave., Suite 311
San Diego, CA 92111
phone: (858) 694-0317
website: http://nasnutrition.com

The NASN is a professional organization of health and fitness professionals dedicated to the field of sports nutrition. The website contains information on obtaining sports nutrition certificates or licenses through a distance-learning program, hosted seminars, or universities or postsecondary schools.

Sports, Cardiovascular, and Wellness Nutrition (SCAN)
3000 Bridge Ave., Suite 4
Cleveland, OH 44113
phone: (216) 503-0053
website: www.scandpg.org

SCAN is part of the of the Academy of Nutrition and Dietetics. Its mission is to help members become national experts and leaders. Its website includes links to nutrition information and professional development. SCAN provides many incentives to student members, including academic and certificate information, peer-to-peer networking, mentoring, internship advice, a graduate student grant, a student award, and free or discounted academic materials.

Sports Event Planner

What Does a Sports Event Planner Do?

Beyoncé performed a musical extravaganza during the 2013 Super Bowl halftime show without a hitch. Shortly after play resumed, however, the stadium was plunged into darkness when the electricity went out. Event planners activated emergency protocols, which included backup generators and notifying community officials. Thirty-four minutes later the lights and the game were back on. Although few event planners work on sports events of this scale, the Super Bowl incident illustrates a central tenet of this career: be ready for anything.

From college tennis matches to a city marathon to the Olympics, sports event planners organize and promote athletic games and tournaments. Planners often work with athletes and celebrities. They handle all of the logistics and details to ensure the event is successful. While the planner's duties depend on the event size, venue, and em-

---

At a Glance:

Sports Event Planner

Minimum Educational Requirements
Bachelor's degree

Personal Qualities
Organized; excellent communication skills

Certification and Licensing
Voluntary

Working Conditions
Indoors and outdoors

Salary Range
About $25,940 to $82,060

Number of Jobs
As of 2012, about 94,200 for all event planners

Future Job Outlook
Better than average

58

ployer, all planners have a limited budget. They keep the budget in mind as they select and negotiate the cost of the venue, hire and manage workers, and order supplies and materials needed to ensure the event runs smoothly. They also may supervise ticket and concession sales, interact with media and handle publicity, and inspect the facility. For away games, planners might also organize and purchase team lodging and transportation and take care of other travel expenses.

Some sports event planners work full time for a college or professional sports team. Others work for a sports recreation center or camp, booking events for their facility. For example, Sue Harsharger, a sports event planner at the Eugene, Cascades & Coast Sports Commission, organized Oregon's winter games for the Special Olympics. Others work for event planning companies and are hired by businesses, gyms, and nonprofit organizations to organize community events like fun runs, golf tournaments, and tennis matches.

Sports event planners begin by meeting with the client and other personnel to discuss the purpose of the event. Planning a sports event requires teamwork. Planners work with advertising, sales, public relations, creative services, client marketing, legal, security, business offices, and other departments. They plan the scope of the event, which includes the date, time, location, and budget. They identify all of the tasks, personnel, and supplies needed for the event. Meetings are held throughout the planning process, and the planner must take meticulous notes on decisions made at the meetings as well as items that require additional research or action. They create a master plan of action, identifying all of the tasks required for the event. This plan includes milestones or due dates for each task along with who will be responsible for each task. Creating emergency contingency plans to deal with potential problems, like the weather, is also part of the planning process. In the article "What It Takes to Host a Super Bowl" on the Connect Sports website, Dawn Reiss writes about the 2014 Super Bowl contingency plan for snow: "At MetLife Stadium, the Super Bowl snow removal plan includes a crew of 1,600 workers, double the typical 800 workers for Giants and Jets games. In the seating areas, a fine-tuned system of snow chutes can direct snow to designated areas where it will then be loaded into Aero snow melters that can melt up to 150 tons of snow per hour."

Large sporting events such as the Boston Marathon (pictured) and smaller sporting events such as a local tennis or soccer tournament require a great deal of planning and organization. This is the work done by sports event planners.

Once the plan is finalized, the event professional tackles all of the jobs. Sports event planners may solicit bids from different vendors to sell food, supplies, and merchandise at the event. These planners might get bids from security companies, janitorial services, photographers, videographers, and other service providers. Planners use spreadsheets or other budgeting software to track expenditures. They also use event planning software, apps, and other tools to organize the event and communicate with their team.

Another important duty is recruiting and managing volunteers. In the article "Engaging Community Volunteers—the Secret to a Successful Sporting Event," posted on the Sports Destinations Management website, Mike Guswiler writes, "In many ways, your volunteer program can be your best asset to elevating your events from average to exceptional—all the more reason to have the best possible volunteer recruitment and management program in place."

The day of the event is often the busiest day for event planners. They work tirelessly to make sure all of their planning and hard work comes to fruition. If problems arise, they implement their contingency plans. Once the event is over, they are likely still at the venue making sure the cleanup crew completes its job. Sports event planners enjoy seeing the participants enjoy the event, knowing their planning made it all possible.

How Do You Become a Sports Event Planner?

Education

To prepare for this career, high school students should take math, speech, English, and business courses. Most sports event planning positions require at least a bachelor's degree from an accredited program, which usually requires four years. Popular majors for this career are sports management, athletic administration, marketing, public relations, communications, or business administration. College-level courses for people who intend to work as sports planners include sports promotion, sports operations, facility management, business law, and sports leadership.

Certification and Licensing

The National Association of Sports Commissions (NASC) offers the sports event executive certification, which is a voluntary certification for sports event planners. To be certified, participants must complete eight modules, have at least five years of experience in the sports tourism industry, and be a NASC member. The modules include these core subjects: strategic planning, event management, technology, revenue generation, and the bid process.

Individuals may also obtain the certified meeting professional credential through the Convention Industry Council. Applicants must have thirty-six months of meeting management experience, recent meeting management employment, and continuing-education credits. To receive the credential, they must pass an exam that covers adult learning, financial management, facilities and services, logistics, and meeting programs.

Volunteer Work and Internships

Volunteers are an integral part of sporting events. Aspiring sports event planners can gain valuable experience by volunteering for youth, amateur, or professional sports teams. Many of these athletic organizations have a volunteer coordinator who will provide training and supervision.

Several sports programs, businesses, and teams offer internships that give college students valuable experiences. The NFL Summer Internship Program provides participants a behind-the-scenes learning experience in a variety of departments, including event planning. During the eight- to nine-week program, interns learn about the business side of professional football from speaker presentations, mentoring partnerships, and networking opportunities. Applicants must be undergraduate juniors with an overall GPA of at least 3.0.

Sports-related internships can be found online. A 2015 search for event planning internships on one website yielded 127 positions, ranging from a pro sports arena operations intern to an assistant to the US Paralympics Sports Performance Team. ESPN offers paid ten-week internships in the fall, spring, and summer semesters to students currently enrolled in a degree program. Interns work behind the scenes with ESPN staff. For example, two ESPN interns participated in the 2015 Special Olympics World Games in Los Angeles.

Skills and Personality

Sports event planners must be organized and detail oriented to plan the project, meet deadlines, and carry out all the tasks required for the event. They must maintain excellent records, including contact information for vendors, meeting notes, expenses, and a detailed project plan. They note all communication with clients, suppliers, and event staff.

These professionals also establish and maintain positive interpersonal relationships with their clients, vendors, and staff. Networking with other event planners helps them foster professional working relationships, which can lead to new business, and helps find the best price and quality in venues, supplies, and other resources. Good people skills also help planners negotiate the best contract prices for their client.

When problems arise, planners must maintain their composure and find creative ways to resolve the situation and satisfy the client. In an interview on Connect Sports, Mary Pat Augenthaler, the vice president of events for the NFL, explains the importance of event planners handling problems calmly. "A key characteristic is being able to think on your feet," she says. "You do everything you can beforehand, but when it comes to execution you have to become the most flexible person in the world."

On the Job

Employers

According to the Bureau of Labor Statistics (BLS), one in six event planners is self-employed. Sports event planners are employed by professional sports organizations, collegiate athletic departments, and youth sports organizations. They may also plan events for health and fitness clubs, country clubs, sporting goods outlets, and non-profit organizations with an athletic focus. Still others are hired by sports event planning or sports marketing companies that are hired by organizations to plan their events.

Working Conditions

Most sports event planners are employed full time and work at least forty hours a week, which often includes weekends, evenings, and long, irregular hours. They attend many indoor office meetings but also travel to the event location to check on progress. When the event is held outside, they work outdoors and may work on their feet most of the time.

Sports event planners are at risk for job stress because their work environment is fast paced and demanding, especially on the day of the event. According to the CareerCast website, event planning is one of the top ten most stressful jobs in America. Having to work with a tight budget, being held to high expectations, and coordinating with many people contribute to job stress.

Earnings

According to the BLS, the average annual salary for all event planners in 2012 was $50,910. It further reports that the average annual salary for promoters of performing arts, sports, and similar events was $47,700. The salaries for this career vary greatly due to the company, job location, industry, benefits package, and the applicant's education and experience. Salaries are often commensurate with job experience. The BLS reports that the highest annual mean wages for this career are offered in the District of Columbia, $68,000; New York, $61,980; Connecticut, $61,630; Massachusetts, $60,350; and Virginia, $57,910.

Opportunities for Advancement

Gaining experience, certification, and education help sports event planners advance their careers. Planners often begin with entry-level positions, performing basic tasks under the supervision of the senior planner. As planners gain experience, they assume greater responsibilities in an organization. Those working for an independent sports planning business will take on larger clients as they advance their careers. For example, they may move up from handling events for a college to planning events for a professional sports team. Earning a master's degree in sports management or a related field can also help planners start and develop a thriving independent consulting business.

What Is the Future Outlook for Sports Event Planners?

The BLS predicts that employment of all event planners will grow by 33 percent, creating 31,300 new jobs by 2022. According to the Sports Management Degree Guide website, the outlook for sports event planners will continue to grow because spectator sports in the United States generate $485 billion each year. The most promising job outlook will be for those with a good education, extensive experience, professional credentials, excellent interpersonal skills, and strong time management skills.

Find Out More

Collegiate Event and Facility Management Association (CEFMA)
24651 Detroit Rd.
Westlake, OH 44145
phone: (440) 892-4000
website: www.nacda.com/cefma/nacda-cefma.html

The CEFMA was founded by the National Association of Collegiate Directors of Athletics (NACDA) in 2008 and is committed to providing educational programs, professional development, and networking opportunities, as well as strategies and tips to improve event and facility management. Its website has links to internships, jobs, awards, conventions, and foundations.

Event Planners Association
25432 Trabuco Rd., Suite 207
Lake Forest, CA 92630
phone: (866) 380-3372
website: http://eventplannersassociation.com

The Event Planners Association is the national trade organization for professionals in the event and amusement industries. This association provides a variety of services to event planners as well as to those seeking their services. Its website offers *The Event Planner's Guide Book*, weekly planner archives, webinars, and training and certification information.

National Association of Sports Commissions (NASC)
9916 Carver Rd., Suite 100
Cincinnati, OH 45202
phone: (513) 281-3888
website: www.sportscommissions.org

The NASC is a membership organization that provides sports event information to those in the sports tourism or sports events industry. The organization also offers the certified sports event executive certification. The NASC website contains information on sports marketing, fund-raising, and other resources to enhance the quality of sports events.

SportsEvents
PO Box 2267
Gulf Shores, AL 36547
phone: (800) 968-0712
e-mail: info@sportseventsmagazine.com
website: http://sportseventsmagazine.com

SportsEvents magazine publishes "how-to" articles to help sports event planners create successful amateur sporting events and competitions. Its website includes previous magazine issues, a convention center guide, surveys, bid sheets, a list of sports, and an "Ask the Experts" link.

Sports Planning Guide
621 Plainfield Rd., Suite 406
Willowbrook, IL 60527
phone: (630) 794-0696
website: http://sportsplanningguide.com

The *Sports Planning Guide* is an annual publication filled with planning tips, sports events strategies, interviews with top industry representatives, and information on top sporting destinations for event planners. A free PDF of the guide as well as numerous articles about planning sports-related events can be downloaded from its website.

Sports Medicine Physician

What Does a Sports Medicine Physician Do?

After Amber, a college softball catcher, suffered a serious knee injury in 2014, Dr. Marc Milia of Beaumont Hospital in Dearborn, Michigan, performed reconstructive surgery on the ligaments in her knee. She made a complete recovery and rejoined her softball team the next spring. Amber is just one of thousands of athletes who, each year, require surgery or other procedures performed by sports medicine physicians. These doctors specialize in the diagnosis and treatment of injuries and other physical conditions that negatively affect athletic performance in professionals and amateurs alike. As Joshua Purses, a sports medicine physician with MultiCare Orthopedics & Sports Medicine, explains on the organization's website, "A large portion of my patients are active adults and children, 'weekend warriors,' 'industrial athletes,' or even those who are not physically active but have orthopedic issues." Sports medicine doctors

At a Glance:

Sports Medicine Physician

Minimum Educational Requirements
Doctor of medicine or doctor of osteopathy degree

Personal Qualities
Dedicated; compassionate

Certification and Licensing
Medical license; certification in sports medicine

Working Conditions
Indoors and outdoors

Salary Range
About $173,431 to $364,589

Number of Jobs
As of 2012, about 349,000

Future Job Outlook
Better than average

generally focus on joint, bone, and muscle health, including acute injuries such as ankle sprains, joint injuries, dislocations, and nonsurgical fractures; overuse injuries, including stress fractures, tendonitis, and osteoarthritis; and traumatic brain injuries or concussions.

Sports medicine physicians specialize in either surgical care (surgical repair of damaged tendons, ligaments, and joints) or primary care (which encompasses all nonsurgical care). While some sports medicine doctors work full time as team physicians, many practice medicine in a hospital, clinic, or private practice during the day and work as a team sports medicine physician in the evening or on weekends. During an interview with the author, John Dawkins, a family practice and sports medicine physician at Scripps Clinic in San Diego, commented, "I work fifty or more hours a week at the clinic and then attend practices and games at the University of San Diego on evenings and weekends."

Sports medicine physicians are employed by college, university, Olympic, and professional sports teams. They work closely with other medical professionals, including athletic trainers and sports dietitians, to keep the team healthy and safe. Preventing injuries is a sports physician's first consideration. Physicians collaborate with sports dietitians to advise athletes on optimal weight, diet, nutrition, and good sleep habits. They also work with personal trainers to develop effective conditioning and exercise programs for athletes. They consult with coaches to ensure protective gear and sports training practices are safe. Sports physicians examine athletes to determine fitness level, identify underlying diseases or injuries, and determine if the player is fit to play. They also examine players for symptoms of alcoholism and substance abuse and monitor and treat players for diseases like diabetes, asthma, and mononucleosis.

Team doctors attend practices and games to provide emergency medical treatment. They select and prepare medical equipment and medications to bring to competitions. When a player is injured, the doctor evaluates the injury to determine if the player is able to return to play or should be pulled from the game. Concussions, broken bones, and deep lacerations are some of the serious injuries requiring immediate care. Sports medicine physicians may order tests, examine X-rays, or review other data to determine the severity of the injury. For example, some sports teams use state-of-the-art football helmets that measure how much force was absorbed during impact and relay the data via telemetry for doctors to review in determining if the player has suffered a concussion. Doctors also determine whether they are able to treat the athlete or need to send the athlete to an emergency room or refer him or her to a surgeon.

Team doctors also oversee the treatment and rehabilitation of injured or sick athletes. They coordinate care with surgeons, nurses, physical therapists, athletic trainers, and other health personnel to ensure the athlete is recovering. It is ultimately the sports medicine physician who makes the final return-to-play decision for the athlete. This is a great responsibility, but it gives the doctor a profound sense of accomplishment to see an injured athlete make a full recovery and return to the sport he or she loves. Despite the many years of training and long work hours, this can be a very rewarding profession. As Dr. Dawkins explains, "The most rewarding part of my job is the positive relationships I form with my patients."

How Do You Become a Sports Medicine Physician?

Education

Life sciences classes such as biology and medical pathway programs, when available, are valuable starting points for high school students who are interested in a career as a sports medicine physician. Other classes that provide good early preparation include anatomy, chemistry, physics, math, and physical education. Taking advanced placement classes in these areas will help prepare students for the academic rigor required to become a doctor.

Becoming a sports medicine physician requires at least ten years of university-level academic coursework and training. The first several years of education and training are the same as for any other medical doctor. The first step is to obtain a bachelor's degree with an emphasis on premedical curriculum, which usually takes four years. Admittance to an accredited medical school is the next step. After obtaining a medical degree, a process that typically takes four years, the graduate completes a residency program lasting two to seven years in fields like surgery, family medicine, emergency medicine, internal medicine, physical medicine and rehabilitation, or pediatrics.

Completing a one- to two-year sports medicine fellowship is the last step in becoming a sports medicine physician. A fellowship is a one-on-one learning experience guided by an attending faculty member. The fellow works with patients who have sports injuries and assists athletes with strength conditioning and injury prevention. For example, in Ohio State University's sports medicine fellowship, the fellow helps with over nine hundred Division 1 NCAA athletes on thirty-six varsity teams. Fellows attend athletic events and give medical care as needed, attend conferences, gain teaching experience, and often complete a research project.

Sports medicine doctors following a surgical route complete a one- to two-year surgical sports medicine fellowship. Surgical fellowships may be generalized or may focus on a specific area of the body, like the shoulder or knee.

Certification and Licensing

Like all doctors, sports medicine physicians must be licensed to practice medicine. To earn a license, applicants must graduate from an accredited medical school, finish a residency program, and pass the US Medical Licensing Examination or the Comprehensive Osteopathic Medical Licensing Examination.

After finishing a sports medicine residency program, a physician earns board certification in the sports medicine specialty from either the American Board of Medical Specialties or the American Osteopathic Association. The American Board of Internal Medicine offers a voluntary professional board certification for sports medicine doctors. After completing a fellowship, a physician may earn a certificate of added qualification in sports medicine.

Volunteer Work and Internships

Volunteer work can be a key component to being accepted into medical school. According to the *US News & World Report* website, "Medical schools like to see that applicants not only know what they're pursuing (i.e., the field of medicine), but also that they've demonstrated some commitment, and ideally some leadership, while they've been undergraduates." Volunteering enables individuals to see if they enjoy work in the medical field, network with peers and mentors, develop leadership skills, and add to their résumés. High school students can find volunteer opportunities by talking to their school's career counselor, checking community service websites, and joining premed or health services clubs at school or in the community. Volunteer positions can also be found by contacting hospitals, clinics, labs, research facilities, charities, foundations, and other organizations.

The National Academy of Future Physicians and Medical Scientists sponsors the Ultimate Med Internship, a seventeen-day hands-on summer program in Ahmadabad, India, where high school students experience real-life gross anatomy labs, operating rooms, and medical treatment rooms. Students work side by side with physicians as they treat patients and perform procedures in the emergency room, outpatient clinics, and medical wards. The program is highly competitive. Tuition includes program costs, international air travel, hotel accommodations, three meals per day, and local transportation.

Skills and Personality

Sports medicine doctors must be willing to complete the years of study, to work long hours, and to be on call twenty-four hours a day to care for patients. Their commitment to patients includes staying up to date on the latest sports medicine technology and information to help their clients achieve peak physical performance, prevent injuries, and recover from sports injuries.

Patients often list compassion and empathy as key traits they look for in a physician. These doctors often examine and treat patients who are in a lot of pain and endure additional pain during the doctor's examination. They also treat patients with potentially life-altering illnesses or injuries. Patients want doctors to be caring, compassionate, and understanding in addition to being skilled and knowledgeable.

Decision making is a critical skill for sports medicine specialists. As team physicians, they assess injured athletes to determine if they are able to continue playing in a game or should be pulled for medical treatment. These doctors must accurately diagnose injuries and decide upon the best treatment options. Because their decisions can have lifelong implications for athletes, they must be cautious but also be able to act quickly.

Sports medicine physicians must have good communication skills. This applies whether they are talking with athletes, trainers, coaches, parents, or other medical providers.

On the Job

Employers

These specialists are employed by amateur, collegiate, Olympic, and professional athletic teams; hospitals and health care clinics; and rehabilitation facilities. They may also be self-employed in private practice or in partnerships with other physicians.

Working Conditions

Regardless of specialty, doctors tend to work irregular and long hours; many work over fifty hours a week. Sports medicine team physicians often work both indoors and outdoors as they oversee training, are on call during games, and diagnose and prescribe treatment for injured athletes. Physicians travel frequently between offices and hospitals to care for patients. Team doctors must also travel to out-of-town sporting events.

Earnings

Salaries for physicians are among the highest of all professions. The 2014 Medical Group Management Association's Physician Compensation and Production Survey reports that sports medicine physicians earn a median annual salary of $222,000. It shows a salary range from $173,431 to $364,589. A sports medicine doctor's earnings vary by location, type of employer, and years of experience. According to the Bureau of Labor Statistics (BLS), as of May 2013 specialty physicians, including sports medicine physicians, earned the highest median income in Mississippi, South Dakota, Montana, Minnesota, and Idaho.

Opportunities for Advancement

Physicians who have accrued years of experience and continuing education often become supervisors, managers, or department directors. Sports medicine physicians working for teams advance by progressing from working at high schools to college to professional or Olympic sports teams.

What Is the Future Outlook for Sports Medicine Physicians?

The BLS predicts that employment for all physicians and surgeons will grow by 18 percent through 2022. This growth is largely due to the expansion of health care industries and because of the increase in the aging population.

Find Out More

American College of Sports Medicine (ACSM)
401 W. Michigan St.
Indianapolis, IN 46202-3233
phone: (317) 637-9200
website: www.acsm.org

The ACSM is an international sports medicine and exercise organization dedicated to improving scientific research, education, and application of exercise science and sports medicine. The website includes career resources, certification information, student awards, student newsletter, and a link to student representatives who provide educational advice.

American Medical Society for Sports Medicine (AMSSM)
4000 W. 114th St., Suite 100
Leawood, KS 66211
phone: (913) 327-1415
website: www.amssm.org

The AMSSM represents sports medicine physicians devoted to education, research, advocacy, and the treatment of athletes. Members specialize in nonsurgical sports medicine, working as team physicians at the youth, professional, and Olympic team levels. The website includes a sports medicine brochure, webinars, and an interactive discussion for physicians and students.

American Orthopaedic Society for Sports Medicine (AOSSM)
9400 W. Higgins Rd., Suite 300
Rosemont, IL 60018
phone: (877) 292-4900
website: www.sportsmed.org

The AOSSM is an international association of orthopedic surgeons and other health professionals dedicated to sports medicine education, research, communication, and camaraderie. Its website has links to an online medical library, sports injury tips, Olympic sports injury resources, a career path brochure, medical questions and answers, and surgical animations.

American Osteopathic Academy of Sports Medicine (AOASM)
2424 American Ln.
Madison, WI 53704
phone: (608) 443-2477
website: www.aoasm.org

The AOASM was founded in 1984 to advance the sports medicine specialty. Its website has a link for students featuring information on residencies and fellowships, news from medical schools, conferences, and awards. There are also links to resources, educational conferences, blogs, and careers.

National Academy of Future Physicians and Medical Scientists
1701 Pennsylvania Ave. NW, Suite 300
Washington, DC 20006
phone: (617) 307-7425
e-mail: support@futuredocs.com
website: www.futuredocs.com

The academy provides free educational programs, a library, mentoring seminars, a social network, and an internship. It also includes information on getting into and paying for college and medical school, college curriculum and summer activities, leadership training, and videos.

Interview with a Recreational Therapist

Melissa Pavlowsky is a certified therapeutic recreational specialist at the Children's Institute in Pittsburgh, Pennsylvania. She has worked as a recreational therapist (RT) for six years and specializes in treating clients with traumatic injuries. Pavlowsky answered questions about her career by e-mail and telephone.

Q: Why did you become a recreational therapist?

A: I went into college undecided. I knew I didn't want a desk job, and I wanted to help people. My adviser recommended recreational therapy classes. The professors were passionate about helping others. They took us to observe recreational therapy programs in a variety of settings. We had many opportunities to see how the coursework was applied in real work settings, which was a very positive experience.

Q: Can you describe a typical workday?

A: My workdays are always different. I work in a hospital treating traumatic injury clients, who have vastly different abilities than before the injury. My patients typically have a brain, spinal cord, or orthopedic injury and spend two to three months at the hospital before they are discharged. My day begins attending a treatment team meeting with the doctors, nurses, psychologist, physical therapists, occupational therapists, and speech therapists. The team discusses each patient's current status, goals, and discharge plans.

I treat six to eight patients a day. My sessions are usually thirty minutes long and focus on a leisure skill they are interested in. I help them work through physical and emotional barriers.

While I mainly see clients individually, I use group therapy when I have patients who are around the same age and have similar medical conditions. When I had three teen boys with spinal cord injuries, we started a lunch group that met at the hospital or a restaurant. We started lunch with what happened during the week, good or bad, and ended with a goal for the week. At first, I was worried they might be jealous of one another's progress and abilities because they all had different levels of movement. However, they encouraged one another and formed a tight support network. When one boy was able to shrug his shoulders, they celebrated his success. When another was able to pick up a french fry, they cheered him on to pick up another. I always advocate that my clients learn the most from their peers.

Q: What do you like the most and least about your job?

A: What I like the most is seeing a positive change in my patients. They come from a traumatic, life-changing event like a car accident, and I help them focus on their abilities, not their disabilities. My patients are what keep me going.

What I like least is the lack of knowledge about the career. At my hospital, the staff understands my job and its importance, but when I meet other RTs at conferences, they say their coworkers or employers don't understand the job. It is a growing career, and as people get to know about it, they understand its value.

Q: What personal qualities do you find valuable for this type of work?

A: It is vital to have empathy. Clients are dealing with life-changing medical conditions, and while I can't know exactly how they are feeling, I need to be sensitive and understanding to their challenges.

Flexibility is also important because schedules change on a daily basis. I've had an outdoor activity planned but discovered the child is stuck in bed because of a medical issue. I've had community outings planned, but the van won't start. When I began working, I didn't know how to handle changes, but I have learned to roll with it. You also have to be able to change your plans to accommodate a patient's interests. I had a recreational therapy student who created a plan for a teenager, but the teen wanted to color a poster. I assured my student that any time a client has another idea, as long as it is a positive choice and helps with their treatment plan, to let the patient take the lead. Ultimately we want clients to take charge of their own leisure activities and lead active lives.

RTs also have to have excellent communication skills. They must carry themselves as professionals and give progress reports to the therapy team. RTs work with clients of all ages and different cognitive abilities, so they must be able to explain the activity and its importance to the child and parent in a way that each can understand. For example, Wii bowling is a fun game, but it also helps the patient improve posture and develop fine and gross motor skills.

This is a very creative career and can be a lot of fun. I rarely do the same intervention on the same day.

Q: What advice do you have for students who might be interested in this career?

A: Observe and get as much volunteer work as possible. I learned a lot visiting different recreational therapy settings. I volunteered at the Children's Institute, which gave me hands-on experience. It also let the hospital get to know me and my passion for the profession, which led to them hiring me after I graduated.

Other Jobs in Sports and Fitness

Adaptive sports coordinator
Agent
Announcer
Biochemist
Biomechanist
Cardiac rehabilitation specialist
Chiropractor
Exercise physiologist
Groundskeeper
Gym manager
Health coach
Kinesiologist
Occupational therapist
Physical therapy assistant
Professional athlete
Scout
Sports accountant
Sports analyst
Sports book ticket writer
Sports engineer
Sports entrepreneur

Sports equipment manager
Sports equipment repair
  technician
Sports information director
Sports journalist
Sports marketing
Sports massage therapist
Sports official
Sports photographer
Sports psychologist
Sports retail sales
Sports security
Sports statistician
Sports videographer
Sportswear designer
Strength and conditioning
  trainer
Tactical strength and
  conditioning facilitator
Team owner
Vendor

Editor's note: The online *Occupational Outlook Handbook* of the US Department of Labor's Bureau of Labor Statistics is an excellent source of information on jobs in hundreds of career fields, including many of those listed here. The *Occupational Outlook Handbook* may be accessed online at www.bls.gov/ooh.

Index